MW01139280

EXTRAORDINARY RECIPES FROM

PITTSBURGH CHEF'S TABLE

LAURA ZORCH, SARAH SUDAR,
AMANDA MᶜFADDEN & JULIA GONGAWARE
Photography by Cayla Zahoran

THE STEEL CITY

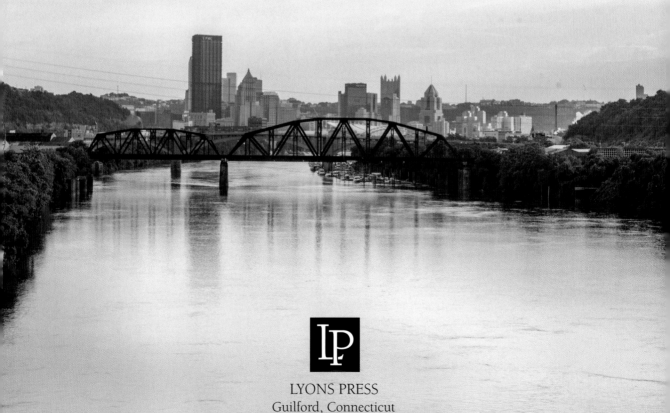

LP

LYONS PRESS
Guilford, Connecticut

An imprint of Globe Pequot Press

Copyright © 2013 Morris Book Publishing, LLC

Lyons Press is an imprint of Globe Pequot Press.

All photography by Cayla Zahoran except those on pages 46 and 49 by ADAM MILLIRON/MILLIRON STUDIOS

Waffles INCaffeinated™ and The Benny™ on pages 196 and 198 are trademarked by Waffles INCaffeinated Co., LLC

Editors: Kevin Sirois and Tracee Williams
Project Editor: Lynn Zelem
Text Design: Libby Kingsbury
Layout Artist: Nancy Freeborn

Library of Congress Cataloging-in-Publication Data is available on file.

ISBN 978-0-7627-9223-8

Printed in the United States of America

10 9 8 7 6 5 4 3 2 1

To Pittsburgh

Contents

Acknowledgments

We at eatPGH have had quite the year, thanks to you. Yes, you, reading this book—you are such a gem! We truly appreciate your support in buying this book, reading our blog, and just being a generally swell human.

We also truly love the city of Pittsburgh. The levels of support we receive from 'Burghers would be unmatched if we were doing what we do in any other town. So, thank you, Pittsburgh. No one compares.

And, of course, this book obviously would not have been possible without the amazing Pittsburgh chefs and restaurant owners. You can't see or hear us right now, but we are giving you a standing ovation complete with catcalls. The work each one of you is doing in this city is applause worthy—and gosh darn it, we are applauding. You are putting Pittsburgh on the map as a place to eat. And a place to eat WELL. Thank you for talking with us, sharing with us, and feeding us.

Finally, a roll call of folks who help us to keep living the dream and keep balling so hard: Kevin Sirois, our editor and fellow mad baller; Tracee Williams, our new friend and coeditor; Cayla Zahoran, photographer extraordinaire; Tom McGraw, cocktail correspondent; Katy Zeglen, recipe tester and baker bud; Sally Turkovich Wright, recipe testing wiz; and Patrick Finan, Brandon Davis, Ben Siegel, David Horesh, Patrick Simons, and Sean Wrafter, our dapper Buffalo gents. Yinz are amazing!

Julia: For Bobby, my best friend, my partner in crime, and my little brother. Without you, life would be boring and I most likely would have starved to death by now. So thank you. For believing in me. And for being you. Seriously.

Amanda: High-five to my family and honorary family who continue to root for me, both in life and around the dinner table when they need someone to finish the last morsel of anything. And bear hugs to the friends who challenge me to be the best Mandy possible, push me forward when I just want to metaphorically lie down and take a nap (sometimes literally), and make me feel wonderful, so wonderful.

Sarah: To my family and friends, thank you for your constant love and support. Without you, I would be dining alone, quite often. To Julia, Laura, and Amanda, I can't believe we did it again! I truly love you gals, just like the three sisters I never had. To the chefs I've met along this journey, thank you for opening up your kitchens and your hearts, and sharing your stories and passion. You totally rock, and I'm glad to call you my new friends!

Laura: Many thanks to my parents for being the best. Really. I'm serious. The best. Going out to dinner would sometimes be impossible without the extra cash they hand me when I pass home—just like Monopoly. Plus, they are just fantastic people. So, thank you, Mom and Dad, for continually keeping my belly—and my heart—full.

Introduction

Pittsburgh is easy to love.

It isn't sexy. No white sand beaches or glitterati. Just three rivers and folks who will hold the door open for you.

It isn't fancy. No $100 million apartments or steak coated in gold leaf. Just abodes with solid views on firework night and grass-fed beef.

It is Pittsburgh. This charmer is a city behaving like a small town, with familiar faces at every turn. The co-worker: "Her father is my dentist." The neighbor: "His cousin sat behind me in eighth-grade homeroom." The bus driver: "We played deck hockey together last Tuesday." Pittsburgh is easy to love because you are always surrounded by friends or soon-to-be pals.

In recent years, this Pittsburgh love has spread. Media praise rains down on the 'Burgh, touting the city as the place to be, visit, live, work, play, and everything else in between. Visitors are shocked to see the city isn't covered in steely smoke (apparently these people only visit once every three decades) and that cool people live here not against their will. Technology happens here. Art thrives in neighborhoods. Let's just be real: Pittsburgh is so hot right now.

So what happened? How did we get here? Pittsburghers ask this question from time to time. The city was turned on its head when the steel industry crashed and burned.

Jobs were lost. Pittsburgh's identity as a titan of industry was lost. All hope, however, was not lost. The spirit of the people here is too strong to break. There was reevaluating and readjusting. It took time (decades). It took patience (plenty). And right now, even as the rebuilding continues, the city is bomb dot com.

The culinary landscape helps to bolster Pittsburgh's new image. Restaurants are sprouting and blossoming, reenergizing neighborhoods and palates. Pittsburgh is no longer a one-sandwich town. Neighborhoods like East Liberty, Downtown, Lawrenceville, and Highland Park are now dining destinations. National spotlights, from *Bon Appétit* to the James Beard Foundation, are shining on the kitchens. Pittsburgh is cooking, quite literally and figuratively.

Remember how we said everyone knows everyone in the 'Burgh? This remains a constant in the Pittsburgh chef community. The love and respect shared is palpable. While competition is a fact of life, the chefs choose to celebrate the successes of others and offer support in any way possible.

As we started our research, we did not anticipate learning about this communal pride of the chefs nested amongst the three rivers. We would often get the question during chef interviews: "So is [insert any number of names here] going to be included in your book? Because he [or she] is doing amazing work." What's more, the large majority of folk represented in the pages herein are buddies, not just admirers of excellent work. Collaborations pop up, much to the delight of every taste bud in town, like Root 174's Keith Fuller churning out tacos on the PGH Taco Truck, and Cure's Justin Severino cooking up meals at Bar Marco during No Menu Mondays. Working together, the chefs

of Pittsburgh's finest food destinations are heightening the level of culinary offerings in the city and making Pittsburgh the tastiest it has ever been. And it is only the beginning. Change is happening. Right here and right now.

"I'm getting goose bumps," observed Chef Brian Pekarcik of Spoon as he summarized the culinary scene. "Being a Pittsburgh native, it's so refreshing to be a part of this organic culture that is being created within the restaurant community."

So what's for dinner in the 'Burgh? All things: Comfort food. Experimental food. Ethnic food. And, across the board: fresh food. Pittsburgh chefs are loving up on the farm-to-table movement, sourcing local produce and meats at every possible chance. Being geographically surrounded by farmland certainly doesn't hurt this quest.

We love the farm-to-table concept—who doesn't want to know where their food is from? We do, sure, but we really want to know who is creating the fare that makes Pittsburgh taste great. So allow us to usher in the new trend in dining (drum roll please): friend-to-table.

On the pages that follow, we will introduce you to over eighty of the finest chefs and restaurateurs in the city, from fifty different restaurants. The men and women interviewed, who raved about one another and praised this fair city, are all different kinds of awesome. These are folks you should know. They are magicians in the kitchen and community revitalizers. They are a group with outsize hearts and big dreams. They shared their stories with us, so now we can share them with you. The history, the inspiration, and the perspiration are spelled out so we might all gain a greater appreciation for the hands crafting delicious dish after delicious dish. They even share some kitchen secrets and recipes you can try at home.

So continue on, dear reader, and meet your new friends.

The chef: "That's my bud."

How to Use This Book Like a Champ

"Hi friend! We want you to make the best use of this book!" Who are "we"? We are eatPGH: Julia Gongaware, Amanda McFadden, Sarah Sudar, and Laura Zorch. We love to eat and eat well. If at any point you have a question about a restaurant or recipe featured in this tome, look us up at eatPGH.com, and we can help you out. We love to talk and talk to you.

We have been dining out in Pittsburgh and writing about it since 2009. So we know what is up. We talked to fifty of the hottest dining establishments in the 'Burgh—at the moment—and got the inside scoop, just for you.

Our friends took time out of their crazy schedules to chat about the who, what, when, where, and why of opening a restaurant, cheffing it up, and being pillars in the community. The best part? They also provided a recipe, or two or three, for you to try at home. These recipes best exemplify the hard work of each chef and restaurateur. A nice mix of recipes—from easy-to-prepare to "what is happening here?!" difficulty levels—are presented after each restaurant's introduction. The recipes provided also represent a variety of courses including appetizers, entrees, desserts, and cocktails.

If you have been searching for a way to impress your friends, now is the time to host a dinner party and make some mackerel (Fukuda's Saba with Grilled Cucumber Foam & Pickled Apple Fluid Gel on page 88) served with a fancy pants drink (Franktuary's Ginzer on page 82), or some other delectable combination.

Since we bet you aren't planning on feeding dozens or hundreds of folk, all of the recipes have been scaled down for home preparation. Most recipes will feed four to eight people. Cocktail recipes are for one. All of this information is spelled out before each recipe, so take note before you start cooking.

Make sure to enjoy your kitchen experiments. And remember, you can always make a reservation.

Happy eating!

STEEL CITY

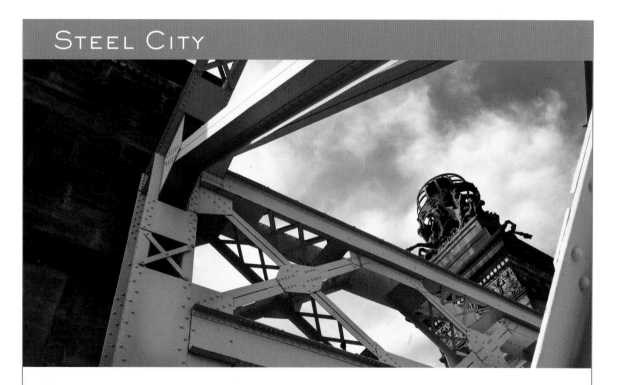

So what's the deal with steel? Pittsburgh's nickname, "The Steel City," was coined because the steel industry was the main economic driver of the 'Burgh for decades. Pittsburgh was built on steel, but the mills are now long gone. The smoky skies have cleared. While physical evidence of this industrial past has vanished, Pittsburgh continues to be proud of its hardworking, rugged past. Want more information about Pittsburgh's steel heritage? Visit Rivers of Steel National Heritage Area, riversofsteel.com.

1947 Tavern

5744½ Ellsworth Avenue
Pittsburgh, PA 15232
(412) 363-1947
1947tavern.com
Chef: Shawn Bain
Bar Manager: Wes Shonk

It started with a toaster. But not just any toaster. A broken toaster. You see, 1947 Tavern's bar manager, Wes Shonk, couldn't own a toaster for longer than two years before it would break. He was frustrated by this simple device that was destined to malfunction. "Why would you design something to break?" he muses. "I found my passion standing over that last broken toaster. I realized I want to produce an incredible product."

Enter 1947 Tavern. The bar and restaurant specializes in classic craft cocktails and American comfort food. "We want to do things the right way," Wes says. "We don't want to cut any corners." The bar menu features traditional drinks like the Sazerac and a long list of over fifty bourbons. Wes has spent countless hours perfecting each sip and keeping on mission to respect bartending's illustrious past.

Chef Shawn Bain thankfully has better luck than Wes with kitchen devices. His foray into his culinary career began with some interesting concoctions from grandma. "I would spend a lot of time with my grandma as a kid," Shawn reminisces. "She would give us cereal dipped in butter." This odd combo, while not exactly tasty, was comforting. You won't find cereal and butter on the 1947 menu, but you will find other dishes to fill your heart and stomach. Favorites include the macaroni and cheese with short ribs and the turkey potpie.

1947 Tavern is named for the year in which its sister restaurant, The Elbow Room, opened its doors. This historical mindfulness echoes throughout the restaurant from those time-honored cocktails to the old-timey tavern atmosphere. Because, in the end, if it isn't broke, don't fix it. And if it is broke, it is probably Wes's toaster.

Maple Spiced Nuts

Makes 8 Cups

For the mixed nuts, anything works, but Shawn usually uses almonds, cashews, peanuts, and Brazil nuts.

1 ounce (¼ stick) unsalted butter
8 cups mixed nuts
½ tablespoon cayenne pepper
½ tablespoon chili powder
⅜ teaspoon kosher salt
⅜ teaspoon ground ginger
½ teaspoon paprika
½ teaspoon pepper
2 cups maple syrup

Preheat oven to 350°F. Grease a 9 x 13-inch pan.

Melt the butter in a saucepan over medium heat. Add the mixed nuts and sauté for 5 minutes.

Add cayenne pepper, chili powder, salt, ginger, paprika, and pepper into the pan. Turn the heat to high and continue to sauté until you can smell the spices cooking (about 4 to 5 minutes). Add the maple syrup, stirring to make sure all of the nuts are coated. Keep the heat on high, stirring occasionally. The nuts will become hard to stir as the syrup is heated. When this happens, pour the nuts onto the greased pan and spread them out in an even layer. Bake for 5 to 10 minutes, until the nuts are golden brown. Check the nuts frequently; there is a fine line between done and burnt!

Let the nuts cool, then enjoy.

MAPLE WHISKEY SOUR

MAKES 1 COCKTAIL

For the perfect party pairing for your spiced nuts, try a Maple Whiskey Sour. Impress your friends with this tasty twist on a classic cocktail.

2 ounces bourbon (Old Grand Dad
    Bonded Bourbon preferred)
¾ ounce pure maple syrup
¾ ounce orange juice
¾ ounce lemon juice
1 egg white (optional)
Ice
Orange slice, for garnish

Pour all of the ingredients (except the orange slice) into a cocktail shaker. Add ice and shake furiously. Strain into a rocks glass over ice. Garnish with an orange slice.

ALLA FAMIGLIA

804 EAST WARRINGTON AVENUE
PITTSBURGH, PA 15210
(412) 488-1440
ALLAFAMIGLIA.COM
CHEF/OWNER: JONATHAN VLASIC
SOUS CHEF: MARK MCMANUS

Growing up, Jonathan Vlasic had the privilege of eating some of the best food of his life: simple, Italian cuisine prepared by his grandparents, mother, and four aunts. Today his family has not only influenced the flavors of his menu at Alla Famiglia but also his attitude as a chef. "My family would never think of not making everything and anything from scratch," says Jonathan. "Here, we make everything. We have to, or it isn't our food."

After seventeen years of experience working in kitchens and a brief stint as a demonstration chef for a food purveyor company, Jonathan purchased Alla Famiglia in 2005 from the previous owner, David Ayn, of Davio in Beechview. Jonathan says he and his predecessor have many things in common: they are both Italian, both formally trained as chefs, and both lifers. "I'm going to be ninety years old and still doing this, just like him."

The menu changes daily, featuring twelve items every night. Proteins such as goat, lamb, boar, fish, and veal are on constant rotation to keep things interesting and keep customers coming back for more. And come back they do for the softball-size mozzarella-cheese-stuffed meatball appetizer and the salt, pepper, and olive oil pasta tossed and served tableside in a cheese wheel. Yes, a wheel of cheese. Jonathan says that even if a customer favorite isn't on the menu, he can probably make it and about thirty other staples that regulars have come to know and love.

Before Jonathan, Alla Famiglia was a five-table restaurant serving great Italian food. With Jonathan and his team in the kitchen, the restaurant is still doing just that, but with more tables, a cocktail lounge, and an outside patio. And on the horizon, Jonathan is looking to expand Alla Famiglia even more—into the space next door—and make it "one of the best restaurants this city has ever seen."

Benvenuti Alla Famiglia

*Mio padre mi ha insegnato le cose che io insegno ai miei figli;
onore, rispetto, tradizione—cento anni alla famiglia!*

"My father teaches me lessons I teach my family;
honor, respect, tradition—100 years to the family!"

—Alla Famiglia proverb

La Pasta alla Bolognese dall'Umbria

PASTA BOLOGNESE FROM UMBRIA

SERVES 8–12 (OR A LARGE FAMILY WITH LEFTOVERS)

1 pound pork shoulder, finely ground
½ pound lamb, finely ground
½ pound beef, finely ground
Olive oil (a few tablespoons)
Salt and freshly ground pepper to taste
¼ cup celery, diced into ⅛-inch pieces
1 cup onions, diced into ⅛-inch pieces
¼ cup carrots, diced into ⅛-inch pieces
½ cup heavy cream
64 ounces plain tomato sauce
1½ cups water, plus more as needed
½ cup white wine (a medium-bodied blend
    preferably from Umbria)
1 tablespoon fresh thyme leaves,
    stems removed
10 medium sage leaves
8–12 servings cooked pasta of your choice

In a saucepan over medium heat, lightly brown the ground pork shoulder, ground lamb, and ground beef in olive oil, breaking them up with a spatula into small morsels. As the meats are browning, lightly season with salt and pepper to taste.

Once meat is broken up, add in diced celery, onions, and carrots. Lightly sweat the vegetables with the meat until tender. Reduce heat to low and add in heavy cream.

Next, add plain tomato sauce and water and stir well. Add white wine and simmer on very low heat for a minimum of 1 hour. (*Note:* You may add more water during the reduction process as the sauce simmers.) The pink sauce will give way to a rich, red color through the simmering process. Once complete, add the thyme and sage at the very end. Add more salt if desired.

Toss sauce with cooked pasta of your choice, preferably a fresh semolina product.

Note from the chef: Chef Jonathan says this is a nice sauce to make ahead of time and freeze in portioned containers for impromptu dinner guests.

Trifolata con Funghi

WILD FOREST MUSHROOMS IN A SWEET MARSALA CREAM

SERVES 4–6, ANTIPASTO STYLE

¼ cup dark and golden raisins

6 tablespoons sweet Marsala wine,
plus additional for steeping the raisins

1 cup (2 sticks) unsalted butter

1 pound assorted mushrooms (white, shiitake,
portabello, crimini, oysters, etc.),
cleaned and thickly sliced

2 tablespoons light brown sugar

1 teaspoon granulated sugar

9 ounces heavy cream

Crusty bread, for serving

To prepare raisins: The day before you make the sauce, steep raisins in hot water with a shot of sweet Marsala wine. Refrigerate overnight.

To clarify butter: Heat unsalted butter in a saucepan over low heat until melted. Simmer on low until foam rises to the top. Once the foam has risen, remove the saucepan from the heat. Skim off foam with spoon. Strain the remaining butter through a mesh strainer.

To prepare the sauce: In a large sauté pan on medium-high heat, add clarified butter and mushrooms. Sauté until the mushroom are tender. Once the mushrooms are tender, deglaze the pan with Marsala wine, using a spatula to scrape the bottom of the pan. Add brown sugar, granulated sugar, and raisins, and reduce until the pan is almost dry of all liquid. Add cream and reduce further until the sauce is thick enough to coat the back of a spoon.

To serve: Place in a bowl and serve with crusty bread and other antipasti.

Avenue B

5501 Centre Avenue
Pittsburgh, PA 15232
(412) 683-3663
avenueb-pgh.com
Chef/Owner: Chris Bonfili
Owner: Jenn Bonfili

A chalkboard menu. That was Chef Chris Bonfili's first step in bringing his vision for Avenue B to life. It would allow his menu to be flexible enough to evolve every day while also making it a conversation starter for his staff and anyone who was curious enough about the intoxicating smells wafting through the dining room.

Being in the kitchen is in Chris's blood. His grandmother ran the kitchen of a local restaurant for sixty years, and his dad and uncle were cooks in the International Guard. It wasn't until after culinary school and time working for two James Beard award–winning chefs out West that Chris fell in love with food and saw what it could become for him. "You work in great kitchens for great chefs, and you see that everybody is on board. You don't have anyone in these kitchens just there for a paycheck. Seeing that it can be an entire team of people striving toward a common goal really stuck with me," says Chris.

He brought this passion back to the 'Burgh and set out to bring it alive. It started with finding the right space. The kind of space that would fit chalkboard menus.

There are two menus at Avenue B: a seasonal printed menu and the daily chalkboard. The printed menu includes three starters and three entrees. Two staples on it since the beginning are the fish-and-chips and Kobe meat loaf. The chalkboard menu follows a format: two seafood options, two red meat options, a vegetarian option, and two entrees that can range from rabbit to pasta. Chris completes the chalkboard menu each day around 3 p.m. with a few things in mind: keeping it well-rounded, incorporating flavors that appeal to everyone, and a colorful presentation.

It's that attention to detail that keeps Chris's vision fresh, evolving, and on point. "Never take a night off, never take a dish off. It might be cliché but you're only as good as the last dish you plate."

Butternut Squash Green Chili

SERVES 8–10

5 pounds butternut squash

Light blended olive oil

Salt and black pepper to taste

2 medium-size yellow onions, cut into medium dice

6 ribs celery, cut into medium dice

2 tablespoons (¼ stick) unsalted butter

1 tablespoon ground cumin

1 tablespoon Spanish paprika

1 teaspoon ground cayenne pepper

2 quarts vegetable stock, plus additional for thinning the soup, if desired

½ cup heavy cream

¼ cup chopped fire-roasted poblano peppers

Special equipment:

Blender

Preheat oven to 375°F.

Split the squash lengthwise and place on a baking sheet. Drizzle squash with light olive oil, salt, and black pepper. Roast in oven until soft, approximately 40 minutes. Remove from the oven and allow squash to cool.

In a heavy-bottomed soup pot, sweat onions and celery in 2 tablespoons butter over medium heat until translucent. Add dried spices and stir constantly until aromatic, about 2 minutes. Next add vegetable stock and heavy cream and bring to a simmer.

While soup is coming to a simmer, scrape out the seeds and peel the skin from the roasted squash; discard. Add the squash flesh to the soup pot. Once squash is in the pot, allow to simmer for about 20 to 25 minutes. Remove from heat and allow to cool slightly. After soup has cooled, blend on high until soup is silky smooth. Season to taste with salt and pepper and add the chopped poblano peppers. Adjust the heat and spiciness of the soup with the amount of peppers you use. Additional vegetable stock can be used to thin soup if it is too thick.

POTATO GNOCCHI WITH FAVAS & CRISPY PROSCIUTTO
SERVES 6–8

6 russet potatoes
Kosher salt
3 whole eggs
1½ cups all-purpose flour, plus additional
    for rolling out gnocchi
Pinch of ground nutmeg
¼ pound prosciutto, sliced
2 tablespoons olive oil for prosciutto
1 tablespoon unsalted butter
½ yellow onion, diced small
¼ pound fava beans, shelled and blanched
¼ cup chicken stock or white wine
Salt and pepper to taste
¼ cup chopped fresh mint for garnish (optional)

Special equipment:

Food mill
Stand mixer with dough hook

Preheat oven to 350°F.

Bake potatoes on a bed of kosher salt for about 1 hour until soft. Split potatoes open and cook for an additional 15 minutes. Allow the potatoes to cool for a few minutes just until they can be handled but are still hot. Scoop out the potato flesh and pass it through a food mill into the bowl of a stand mixer.

Add eggs, flour, and nutmeg to potatoes. Mix with a dough hook on medium-high until all ingredients are loosely incorporated. Do not overmix. The dough should still be warm at this point. Divide dough into 5 to 7 smaller balls and place on a floured table. Gently roll the dough into logs with the diameter of a quarter. From there, cut each log into 1½-inch sections. Place a piece of dough on the back of a fork, press your thumb lightly into dough, and roll the dough off fork, leaving a thumb print on one side and lines from the fork on the other side. Repeat with the remaining pieces of dough.

Blanch gnocchi in boiling salted water until they float. Allow to float for 2 minutes. Remove from water and set on an oiled baking sheet to cool.

In a medium-size skillet, crisp the sliced prosciutto in olive oil, remove from the pan, and set aside; prosciutto can be broken apart once it is crispy. Add 1 tablespoon of butter and desired amount of gnocchi to the pan. Sauté over medium-high heat until the gnocchi start to brown slightly. Add diced onion and continue to sauté until onion is translucent. Next, add blanched fava beans and a splash of white wine or chicken stock. Season with salt and pepper. Add crispy prosciutto and serve. Garnish with fresh mint, if desired.

Note from the chef: Extra gnocchi will hold in refrigerator, covered, for 24 hours.

Bar Marco

2216 Penn Avenue
Pittsburgh, PA 15222
(412) 471-1900
barmarco.squarespace.com
Owners: Kevin Cox, Bobby Fry, Michael Kreha,
and Justin Steel

Justin Steel had a daily routine that started at 2:30 a.m. A fourth of the ownership team and a chef in the kitchen, Steel worked in finance even as Bar Marco welcomed its first visitors in early 2012. Trading on European hours and finishing the "work" day at 2 p.m., he trekked from Downtown to the restaurant's home in the Strip, stopping at local purveyors for ingredients to incorporate into dishes that same evening.

A man. A suit. And his fresh produce.

While no longer pounding the pavement from work to work, the four high school friends behind Bar Marco—Justin, Bobby Fry, Michael Kreha, and Kevin Cox—run on all cylinders at all times. This enthusiasm and energy runs deep. Bobby and Michael lived large in New York City, planning all-night dinner parties, before returning to the 'Burgh to create a place for good food paired with good drink.

It is more than appropriate that the oozing-with-hip haunt opened its door on one of the biggest party nights of the year: New Year's Eve. Pittsburgh's former No. 7 Engine Company, lovingly restored by the four gents, has remained a happening hot spot since night one. Echoes of the boozy and electric NYC nights pulse through the air of the intimate bar space on the first floor, where the guys sling craft cocktails paired with small plates of food, such as chili goat-cheese fries and quail yolk ravioli. And upstairs, a private event space displays local artisans' work.

Listen closely to hear the Bar Marco heartbeat: thump-thump, awesome.

And this Bar Marco heart is actually quite big. Every Monday, the restaurant hosts No Menu Mondays for emerging and established chefs to get creative in the kitchen and keep the profit. As Bobby says, "You have to be a part of something bigger and play a small part in it. You have to help each other."

And, sometimes, you need to match a good pair of walking shoes to your business suit.

Rhubarb Glaze

MAKES 2 CUPS

2 pounds rhubarb, chopped
1 teaspoon salt
½ cup light brown sugar
1 cup apple cider vinegar
⅛ teaspoon ground cayenne pepper
⅛ teaspoon ground cumin
1 cup chicken stock
Salt and pepper to taste

Special equipment

Blender
Chinois

Bring all ingredients to a simmer in a saucepan and let cook for about 40 minutes.

Puree and pass through a chinois. Adjust seasoning to taste.

Note from the chef: Justin says this glaze is perfect for poultry. At Bar Marco, he uses it on charred quail, as pictured.

Ramp Salsa Verde

SERVES 8

1 pound ramps, finely chopped, keeping white parts
    separate from green
2 shallots, minced
¾ cup parsley, minced
½ cup lemon juice
½ teaspoon crushed red pepper flakes
1½ cups olive oil
1 teaspoon salt, or to taste

Combine all ingredients and adjust seasoning to taste.

Note from the chef: This is a very versatile sauce that can be used to dress grilled red meats or serve as a dipping sauce for fried foods. It is the base for Bar Marco's wild mushroom arancini, as pictured.

FOOD REVOLUTION PITTSBURGH COOKING CLUB

In 2012, Pittsburgh made a one-year pledge to Jamie Oliver's Food Revolution program, the first city in the United States to do so. The commitment: to help make the region healthier. One of several programs helping spread Jamie's mission is an after-school cooking club held at The Barack Obama Academy of International Studies in East Liberty. The program, conceived by Kelsey Weisgerber, food service director of the Environmental Charter School, and Bobby Fry, co-owner of Bar Marco, teaches high school students basic cooking skills in

hopes that they can change the way they eat and prepare foods in their homes. Local chefs are brought into classes and not only demonstrate techniques to the students but also cook meals for them. Follow all of the happenings of Food Revolution Pittsburgh on Facebook at facebook.com/FoodRevolutionPittsburgh.

BLUEBIRD KITCHEN

221 FORBES AVENUE
PITTSBURGH, PA 15222
(412) 642-4414
BLUEBIRDKITCHEN.COM
OWNER: ELIZABETH MOORE PESSARO
EXECUTIVE CHEF: STEVEN THOMPSON
HEAD PASTRY CHEF: JULIE COGLEY

It's hard not to picture chirpy cartoon birds fluttering around a raven-haired, pie-making princess and seven dwarves as you enter Bluebird Kitchen in historic Market Square. The door swings open to reveal a light, airy space with clean lines, a ceiling for days, and the faint scent of pastries wafting past your nose.

Owner Liz Pessaro's vision was to create a homey atmosphere where patrons would be challenged not to fall into food ruts. Her idea sprang from all the home-cooked meals she ate growing up, the kitchen experiments she and her mother endured, and all the lunches she made herself and took with her day after day to her office job in New York City. As she longed to return to the 'Burgh, she began plotting her would-be restaurant, knowing she wanted to serve modern comfort food that would appeal to meat-and-potatoes gents and finicky dieters alike.

With the help of Executive Chef Steven Thompson, a small core menu was born. The specials evolve seasonally, which further exemplifies the ideals of Bluebird: not to

bore your taste buds with the same humdrum sandwiches but to challenge them with adventure, to explore the world of bacon-shallot jam, oven-dried tomatoes, and Champagne vinaigrette.

Once inside, you're enveloped instantly into the warm and welcoming wings of Bluebird Kitchen. You can't help but gravitate directly toward the display of homemade scones, croissants, and muffins that Head Pastry Chef Julie Cogley so lovingly prepares every day. The real magic is that you never know what you're going to happen upon as you press your face against the glass. That means there is always a new confection to take down with your morning coffee.

Open for breakfast, Bluebird offers several alternatives to pastries, including steel-cut oats with additives like nuts and dried fruit, and savory quiches. Bluebird also serves up sweet-potato corned-beef hash, buttermilk biscuits

and sausage gravy, and a fried egg sandwich that puts all other fried egg sandwiches to shame. And if you can sneak away from your cubicle long enough to stand in line for lunch at Bluebird, you can enjoy one of three daily soups, a sandwich from one heck of a lineup, or fresh salads and sides.

CUMIN CARROT SALAD

SERVES 6–8

2 pounds carrots
4 cups orange juice
2 lemons, sliced
½ cup packed light brown sugar
¼ cup olive oil
2 slices fresh ginger
4 whole garlic cloves
2 tablespoons whole cumin seeds
2 tablespoons kosher salt
2 tablespoons peppercorns
2 sprigs cilantro, finely chopped
2 cups arugula leaves
Sea salt to taste
Lemon oil or fresh lemon and olive oil, to taste

Peel and cut carrots on the diagonal into pieces 1-inch thick. On high heat, bring orange juice, lemons, brown sugar, olive oil, ginger, garlic, cumin seeds, salt, and peppercorns to a boil in a large saucepan. When liquid comes to a boil, reduce heat to low, until it is just barely simmering. Add carrots, maintaining low heat, and let simmer for 20 minutes or until carrots are tender.

Turn off heat and let carrots cool in broth. When cooled completely, remove carrots, discarding broth. Add cilantro and arugula. Sprinkle with sea salt and drizzle with lemon oil, if available, or olive oil and a squirt of fresh lemon juice.

Lemon Meringue Bars

MAKES 1 (8 X 8-INCH) PAN / SERVES 9

For the crust:

6 tablespoons (¾ stick) unsalted butter
½ cup light brown sugar
1 large egg
1 cup finely ground graham cracker crumbs
½ cup flour

For the lemon filling:

6 large egg yolks, at room temperature
1 (14-ounce) can sweetened condensed milk
½ cup freshly squeezed lemon juice (from 2–3 lemons)

For the meringue topping:

1¼ cups granulated sugar, divided
2 tablespoons light corn syrup
3 tablespoons water
6 large egg whites, at room temperature

Special equipment:

Stand mixer with paddle and whisk
    attachments (optional)
Pastry brush
Candy thermometer
Butane torch (optional)

Preheat oven to 350°F.

To prepare the crust: In the bowl of a stand mixer or with a handheld mixer, cream the butter and brown sugar together on medium speed. Add the egg, mixing until combined. Reduce speed to low, and stir in the dry ingredients until a dough forms. Pat into the bottom of 8 x 8-inch pan and bake until light golden brown, about 10 minutes.

To prepare the filling: In the bowl of a stand mixer, with the whisk attachment, or with a handheld mixer, beat the egg yolks on high until pale and fluffy, about 2 to 3 minutes. Gradually add the condensed milk and beat until light and fluffy, about 3 to 5 minutes. Scrape down the sides of the bowl and then beat in the lemon juice.

Pour the filling over the crust and bake for about 15 to 20 minutes, or until the filling is set. Remove from oven and place on a wire rack to cool. Once it has completely cooled, cover and refrigerate for several hours or overnight.

To prepare the meringue topping: Bring 1 cup plus 2 tablespoons sugar, corn syrup, and water to a boil, stirring. Wash down side of pan with a wet pastry brush, and cook sugar syrup, without stirring, until a candy thermometer registers 240°F. Meanwhile, beat egg whites on high with a mixer until soft peaks form. Gradually beat in remaining 2 tablespoons sugar. Add sugar syrup to whites in a slow, steady stream down the side of the bowl. Beat on high speed until thick, fluffy, and cool, about 7 minutes.

Spread meringue on top of chilled lemon bar, swirling to form peaks. With a butane torch, torch the meringue to brown, or place in preheated 500°F oven for several minutes, watching to ensure meringue does not burn. Cool meringue and cut into bars.

Chocolate Mousse Tart

MAKES 1 (10-INCH) TART

For the chocolate shell:

1½ cups all-purpose flour
⅓ cup unsweetened cocoa
¼ teaspoon salt
1 cup (2 sticks) unsalted butter,
   at room temperature
¼ cup granulated sugar
1 teaspoon vanilla extract
1 large egg yolk

For the milk chocolate mousse:

8 ounces chocolate, chopped fine
2½ cups heavy cream, divided, plus additional
   for garnish, if desired
4 egg yolks
¼ cup granulated sugar

Fresh berries for garnish (optional)

Special equipment:

10-inch tart pan with removable bottom
Mixer

Preheat oven to 350°F.

To prepare the chocolate shell: In a medium bowl, combine flour, cocoa powder, and salt. Mix until thoroughly combined. Set aside.

In a large bowl with an electric mixer on medium speed, beat together the butter and sugar until light and creamy, about 3 minutes. Add the vanilla extract and egg yolk and beat until smooth, about 1 minute. Reduce the speed to low and slowly add the flour mixture, mixing just until incorporated. Form dough into a disk, wrap with plastic, and refrigerate until firm. Remove dough from refrigerator. Roll into 1/8-inch-thick round (10-12 inches in diameter) and press into pan. Bake for 10 to 12 minutes.

To prepare the milk chocolate mousse: Place the chopped chocolate into medium-size bowl. Heat 1 cup heavy cream in a heavy-bottomed sauce pan until it almost comes to a boil. While heating the cream, beat the egg yolks and sugar together with electric mixer until creamy yellow color. Stir in ½ cup of the hot cream to temper the eggs. Pour the egg mixture into the remaining cream and stir on low heat until the mixture thickens and coats the back of a spoon. Strain the mixture through sieve over the chopped chocolate. Allow the egg mixture to melt the chocolate and stir to combine. Let cool.

After this mixture cools, beat the remaining 1½ cups heavy cream with electric mixer on medium-high speed until stiff peaks form. Gently fold into the chilled chocolate mixture. Pipe or spoon into a prebaked tart shell and chill for at least 2 hours. Decorate with berries or fresh whipped cream, or both.

Braddock's American Brasserie

107 6th Street
Pittsburgh, PA 15222
(412) 992-2005
BRADDOCKSRESTAURANT.COM
Chef: Brian Volmrich
Pastry Chef: Amanda Kate

Brian Volmrich grew up in Pittsburgh's South Hills but spent much of his time up north in the New Kensington area. He was exposed to two vastly different ways of life at a young age and has said, "I saw the top of white collar to the bottom of blue collar." That early exposure would shape Brian over the years.

Brian enrolled in the Pittsburgh Culinary Institute where he excelled in all facets of the program. His journey then took him to the rolling hills of Virginia where he worked alongside Chef Patrick O'Connell in the Inn at Little Washington, a well-respected French restaurant just outside the Washington, D.C., metro area.

Brian calls his time at the Inn and his tutelage with Patrick "a pivotal moment in my career" where he honed his traditional French cooking skills and grew to appreciate the hard work that is required to run a successful restaurant. Along the way, he also learned the art of ice carving, tended herb gardens, and earned the title of sous chef.

He made his way to Pittsburgh with his young family and settled down in the kitchen at Braddock's American Brasserie, where he has created an exceptional dining experience for locals and out-of-towners who find themselves dining at the restaurant inside the historic Renaissance Hotel on 6th Street.

While Braddock's maintains a core menu with basic protein offerings, Brian has the flexibility to change how those dishes are prepared, and he incorporates as many seasonal and locally sourced ingredients and accoutrements as possible. His real talent is revealed in the featured daily specials he presents.

Foraging

Imagine the satisfaction that can come from tracking, hunting, and foraging for your own food.

Pittsburgh has a handful of chefs who take to the woods to see what is hiding in the wild. Chef Brian Volmrich from Braddock's American Brasserie (page 24) and Chef Seth Bailey from The Café at the Frick (page 32) use a combination of carefully illustrated books, and follow tips and tricks of the trade from professional foragers when they head out to explore.

Edible properties are all around us; take a moment to see what is growing from the ground, climbing up a tree, or hanging from a branch. If you want to go on your own food collecting adventure, check out Wild Purveyors (wildpurveyors.com), who can assist you on your journey.

The close proximity to all of Pittsburgh's sports stadiums keeps Braddock's very busy; it is open for breakfast, lunch, and dinner, as well as brunch on Sunday. Folks come from all over the city to nestle down in a cozy booth and enjoy the braised short-rib pierogies and the French onion soup, two of the shop's best sellers.

Brian spends a lot of time concocting dishes at Braddock's and truly enjoys the marriage between cooking and science. When he isn't practicing his skills in the restaurant, he's at home in New Kensington, tending his garden, foraging for mushrooms, and teaching his young children all there is to know about good food, where it comes from, and how to prepare it so it tastes delicious.

CRAB CAKES WITH LEMON AIOLI

MAKES 10 (4-OUNCE) CAKES

For the lemon aioli (makes 1 cup aioli):

2 tablespoons lemon juice (approximately 2 lemons)
¼ teaspoon turmeric
1 cup blended oil, divided (reserve ½ cup to prepare the lemon oil)
2 egg yolks
½ cup lemon oil (instructions below)
1 teaspoon salt
1 teaspoon granulated sugar

For the crab cakes:

½ cup sliced scallions
¼ cup crushed Ritz crackers
¼ cup mayonnaise (Hellmann's preferred)
2 teaspoons Dijon mustard
2 tablespoons extra-virgin olive oil
1 tablespoon Old Bay Seasoning
2 pounds jumbo lump crabmeat
Salt and pepper to taste
Vegetable oil for cooking

4 cups cleaned arugula

Special equipment:

Blender

To prepare the lemon oil: Peel lemons before juicing and combine the peels, turmeric, and ½ cup blended oil into a small saucepan and bring to a boil. Remove from heat and allow to completely cool. The cooling process allows the lemon to infuse the oil.

To prepare the lemon aioli: Once the lemon oil has cooled, strain out the peels and combine with the remaining ½ cup blended oil. Using a blender, combine all remaining aioli ingredients except for the oils and pulse a couple of times. Slowly create an emulsion by adding a thin, steady stream of oil. The finished oil should have the consistency of mayonnaise; adjust with water if necessary.

To prepare the crab cakes: Combine all ingredients except for crabmeat, salt, pepper, and oil in a large mixing bowl. Carefully fold in crab. Season mixture with a small amount of salt and pepper. Create 10 patties with the mixture and sear the crab cakes in a small amount of oil in a pan over medium heat, being careful not to overload the pan. Once both sides are golden brown, transfer to a plate lined with paper towels.

To serve: Place some lemon aioli on the plate, then add the arugula alongside, and top with a crab cake.

BRAISED PORK SHANKS
OVER WHITE BEAN CASSOULET

SERVES 4

For the pork shanks:

4 pork shanks (or a 3-pound pork butt
    if shanks are unavailable)
Salt and pepper to taste
Vegetable oil for cooking
2 quarts prepared demi-glace

For the white bean cassoulet:

1 pound dried cannellini beans, soaked in water
    overnight (see note)
4 strips bacon, cut into lardoons
2 whole carrots, peeled and cut into small dice
1 onion, peeled and cut into small dice
3 stalks celery, peeled and cut into small dice
2 quarts chicken stock
1 bunch flat-leaf parsley, chopped
10 sprigs thyme leaves, picked and chopped
Salt and pepper to taste

Special equipment:

Parchment paper

To prepare the pork shanks: Preheat the oven to
325°F.

Season the shanks liberally with salt and pepper.
In a high-walled pan, add enough oil to cover the
bottom by 1/2-inch, sear the shanks on all sides
until golden brown. Transfer to a roasting pan and
cover with demi-glace, adding water if necessary.
Cover with parchment paper and then foil. Place
in a 325°F oven for 2 to 3 hours. Test after 2
hours. If the meat pulls away from the bone, the
shanks are done. Allow them to cool down to
room temperature before removing them from
the liquid. Reserve the cooking liquid.

To prepare the white bean cassoulet: Discard
the liquid from the soaked beans. In a large pot,
render the bacon. Once browned, add carrots,
onions, and celery, and cook until the onions
are translucent. Add beans and chicken stock.
Bring to a boil, then reduce to a slow simmer and
cook until beans are tender and not chalky. Add
more water if needed to keep the beans covered
during cooking. Finish with chopped herbs and
season with salt and pepper.

To serve: Heat cassoulet until bubbling and pour
it into serving dishes. Top each dish with a pork
shank that was warmed in its cooking liquid. Pour
some of the reserved cooking liquid over the
shank.

Note from the chef: Soak the beans the night
before serving the dish. In a large container,
cover the beans with water by 4 inches and store
them in the refrigerator overnight.

S'MORES

SERVES 6

For the house-made marshmallows (see note):

3 tablespoons gelatin powder
1 cup water, divided into two ½-cup portions
2 teaspoons vanilla extract
4 egg whites
2 cups granulated sugar
½ cup corn syrup
Salt to taste
Confectioners' sugar for dusting

For the graham biscuits:

1 cup all-purpose flour
3½ cups whole wheat flour
1 cup granulated sugar
2 teaspoons baking powder
1 teaspoon baking soda
1 teaspoon salt
½ teaspoon cinnamon
1 cup (2 sticks) cold unsalted butter,
    run through the large holes of a box grater
¼ cup honey
¼ cup molasses
½ cup cold water

For the fluff:

4 egg whites
1 cup and 2 tablespoons white
    granulated sugar, divided
¾ cup corn syrup

For the cayenne chocolate sauce:

¼ cup cocoa powder
½ pound 64% dark chocolate
1 cup water
10 tablespoons granulated sugar
¾ cup corn syrup
Cayenne pepper to taste

For the white chocolate sauce:

10 tablespoons heavy cream
½ cup white chocolate

1 pint best-quality vanilla bean ice cream for serving

Special equipment:

Stand mixer
Parchment paper
Vegetable oil cooking spray
Butane torch

To prepare the house-made marshmallows: In the bowl of a stand mixer, combine gelatin, ½ cup water, vanilla, and egg whites. Whip to form stiff peaks. In a pot, bring the remaining ingredients (except for the confectioners' sugar) to a boil and pour immediately into the mixer while on low speed. Whip ingredients on high speed until cool. Pour onto a 1/2 sheet tray that has been lined with parchment paper and sprayed conservatively with vegetable oil cooking spray. Allow marshmallows to set at room temperature for 24 hours. Once set, dust with confectioners' sugar and unmold from tray. Cover bottom with confectioners' sugar. Cut into 1-inch squares.

To prepare the graham biscuits: Preheat oven to 350°F. Using the pie dough method, combine all the dry ingredients in a mixing bowl. Add butter, honey, and molasses and work quickly into a cornmeal consistency. Add water and form into a ball. Rest the dough for 20 minutes. Place dough ball between two sheets of parchment paper and roll out to 1/4-inch thickness. Cut into 2-inch squares. Bake on parchment-lined baking sheet for 15 minutes.

To prepare the fluff: Whip the egg whites and 6 tablespoons sugar to form stiff peaks. Bring the remaining sugar and corn syrup to a boil in a saucepan and cook over medium heat until the liquid is clear. Remove from heat. Slowly add the warm mixture to the whites while mixer is on low. Mix until cool.

To prepare the cayenne chocolate sauce: In a bowl, combine cocoa powder and chocolate. In a saucepan, bring water, sugar, and corn syrup to a boil until clear. Pour hot mixture over cocoa powder and chocolate. Stir all ingredients until blended. Add cayenne to taste.

To prepare the white chocolate sauce: Scald the heavy cream and pour it over the chocolate. Stir until uniform and smooth.

To serve: Place one graham biscuit on a plate. Top with a scoop of ice cream, then place another graham biscuit on top. Drizzle some of the sauces around the plate. Add a scoop of fluff to the plate and three or four marshmallow squares. Using a butane torch, brown the fluff and the marshmallows.

Note from the chef: Prepare marshmallows 24 hours prior to serving.

The Café at the Frick

7227 Reynolds Street
The Frick Art and Historical Center
Pittsburgh, PA 15208
(412) 371-0600
THEFRICKPITTSBURGH.ORG
Chef: Seth Bailey

Most teenage boys don't even know how to turn on an oven. At thirteen, Seth Bailey was teaching himself how to make *pâte à choux*. Most teenage boys would probably also wonder: "What is *pâte à choux*?" (It is pastry dough used for cream puffs—FYI). "I always knew I wanted to be a chef," says Seth. "My mom had a professional Culinary Institute of America cookbook, so at thirteen and fourteen years old I was making *pâte à choux* and crepes."

After honing his culinary skills at Johnson and Wales in Charleston, South Carolina, Seth is now the chef at The Café at the Frick, creating dishes for a frequently rotating lunch menu focused on local and sustainable produce. The offerings run the gauntlet from mushroom quiche to rattlesnake chili. "I play off of my own experiences," says Seth.

"For example, I had great clam bellies in Maine during a wedding last summer, and I featured them on our menu shortly after. And if I find a mushroom while foraging outside, I'm going to bring it in and use it."

Along with the changing entrees, salads, soups, and daily desserts, The Café features a high tea every day starting at 2 p.m., complete with tea service, scones, and tea sandwiches. Tea is the perfect complement to the grand scenery that surrounds the restaurant. Set in the landscape of the Frick Art & Historical Center, the former home of Henry Clay Frick and current museum, The Café is picture and palate perfect.

"The atmosphere here is amazing," says Seth. "The other day it was snowing, and it was like eating inside of a snow globe."

Borscht

SERVES 8

2 large red beets
Olive oil
Salt to taste
1 large onion, diced
1 carrot, diced
4 ribs celery, diced
1½ cups shredded white cabbage
3 large cloves garlic, sliced thin
1 large russet potato, cut into medium dice
1 (32-ounce) can tomatoes
1 tablespoon fresh thyme
4 cups chicken stock or vegetable stock
½ cup beluga lentils
3 tablespoons chopped fresh parsley
Sour cream for garnish

Preheat oven to 375°F.

Wash the whole beets thoroughly. Place beets in a baking dish with enough water to cover them one-quarter of the way up. Drizzle with olive oil and sprinkle liberally with salt. Bake for 40 minutes. Once cooled, peel and grate the beets.

Place the onions, carrots, and celery in a heavy-bottomed pot and sweat until slightly softened. Add the shredded cabbage and garlic. Sweat for an additional 5 minutes. Add the diced russet potatoes, tomatoes, thyme, stock, and beluga lentils. Cook until the potatoes and lentils are soft. Add the parsley, and grated beets. Adjust the seasoning to taste.

Garnish with sour cream and serve.

SEA SCALLOPS, POTATO LATKES & CREAMED CORN

SERVES 4

For the potato latkes:

4 large russet potatoes
1 large yellow onion
2 eggs, beaten
½ cup flour
1 tablespoon kosher or sea salt
½ teaspoon black pepper
1 cup sour cream
¼ teaspoon nutmeg
Vegetable oil for cooking

For the creamed corn:

6 ears fresh corn
2 cups heavy cream
Salt and pepper to taste

For the scallops:

½ cup (1 stick) unsalted butter
Vegetable oil for cooking
16 large dry sea scallops

Special equipment:

Ring molds

To prepare the potato latkes: Peel and grate the potatoes and onion. Place into a colander and press out all of the liquid.

Place the potatoes and onions into a bowl. Add the beaten eggs, flour, salt, pepper, sour cream, and nutmeg. Blend with a wooden spoon until incorporated.

Heat a large skillet over medium heat. Once the skillet is hot, add just enough vegetable oil to coat the pan. Place ring molds on the hot skillet and fill with the potato mixture to a depth of ¼ inch. Cook molds on each side for 4 to 6 minutes.

To prepare the creamed corn: Cut the kernels away from the cob and place in a saucepan with the heavy cream. Cook on low heat for 20 minutes or until the cream has reduced by half. Adjust the seasoning with salt and pepper.

To clarify butter: Heat unsalted butter in saucepan over low heat until melted. Simmer on low until foam rises to the top. Once foam has risen, remove the pan from heat. Skim off foam with spoon. Strain remaining liquid through a mesh strainer.

To prepare the scallops: Heat a large skillet over medium-high heat. Add the clarified butter and vegetable oil to coat the pan. Once the oil begins to lightly smoke, add the scallops, being careful not to overcrowd the pan. Cook scallops 3 minutes on each side to medium rare.

To serve: Plate and serve the scallops with the latkes and creamed corn.

CARMI FAMILY RESTAURANT

917 WESTERN AVENUE
PITTSBURGH, PA 15233
(412) 231-0100
CARMIRESTAURANT.COM
OWNERS: CARLEEN AND MICHAEL KING

Carleen and Michael King, kitchen connoisseurs and co-owners of Carmi Family Restaurant, never dreamed of opening a restaurant, but luckily life had different plans.

Michael is a classically trained chef. Carleen possesses the soul food traditions of generations. So when the duo started cooking together, magic happened. "Our friends would ask us to cook, and then friends of friends, and then friends of friends of friends," says Carleen. Thus began a catering business, which transitioned to a restaurant and cemented a beautiful relationship. Carleen and Michael married in May 2013, and, naturally, they catered their own wedding.

"Even though we work together, our schedules don't align," Carleen muses. "So it sounds silly, but I seriously will miss him."

It is hard not to feel this love at their cozy spot on Western Avenue in Pittsburgh's Northside. Warmth radiates from the staff, comprised of Carleen and Michael's families and friends, and from the unmatched comfort food. Any item off the menu, be it the perfectly fried chicken resting on a buttery waffle, the too-good-to-be-true macaroni and cheese, or a bowl of creamy chicken and dumpling soup, inspires a major dining crush. Trying to ward off infatuation is futile.

The food here is that good. Even Carleen's grandma, who inspired some of the restaurant's recipes, approved. "My grandma wasn't one to say how proud she was of you, but she actually said the words," says Carleen. "She would just show love through sitting you down and feeding you."

Carleen's grandma was on to something. Head to Carmi. Sit down. Get fed. Feel the love.

Macaroni and Cheese

MAKES 1 (13 X 9-INCH) CASSEROLE

1 pound elbow macaroni

1 pound sharp cheddar cheese, grated

1 pound Colby Jack cheese, grated

1 pound mozzarella or provolone cheese, grated

1 pound Velveeta, cubed

1 cup (2 sticks) unsalted butter

3 eggs, lightly beaten

1 (12-ounce) can evaporated milk

Salt and pepper to taste

Preheat oven to 350°F.

Cook elbow macaroni in a pot of rapidly boiling salted water for 11 minutes. Drain the macaroni and rinse well.

In a large bowl, combine cheddar, Colby Jack, mozzarella or provolone, and Velveeta with the macaroni. Cut the sticks of butter into the mixture. Add eggs and evaporated milk. Stir the ingredients together then add salt and pepper to taste.

Put the macaroni into a 13 x 9-inch greased casserole dish. Bake the macaroni until hot and bubbly, about 40 to 45 minutes.

CASBAH

229 SOUTH HIGHLAND AVENUE
PITTSBURGH, PA 15206
(412) 661-5656
BIGBURRITO.COM/CASBAH
CORPORATE CHEF: BILL FULLER
EXECUTIVE CHEF: ELI WAHL

Bill Fuller is a badass chef. He's hitchhiked around the country. His kitchen war stories easily outshine Anthony Bourdain's. And he's been a major catalyst in changing the Pittsburgh food scene . . . for the better. As the corporate chef of the Big Burrito Group, he has helped introduce Pittsburgh to a diverse variety of cuisine including Caribbean, Mexican, Asian, and Mediterranean.

One Big Burrito Group location especially close to Bill's heart is Casbah. "Casbah is an expression of how I want my guests to feel when I entertain them," explains Bill. "The colors are warm. The lighting is warm. The service is great and friendly. And the food makes people feel good."

Casbah opened its doors in 1995 with Bill taking the chef's reigns. Originally Casbah was supposed to be a larger version of Kaya, the group's Caribbean restaurant in the Strip District. But after an eating research trip to New York City, Bill and the team shifted gears to Mediterranean. It took some time but Bill and his team eventually broke free from the conservative continental food Pittsburghers were used to and introduced Casbah's signature fresh, simple, unpretentious fare.

Some favorites that have been staples on the menu since the beginning are Bill's interpretation of a classic arugula salad, a hearty pork chop with risotto, orecchiette pasta, and the short rib ravioli. While Bill still oversees the entire operation, Eli Wahl is the current executive chef at Casbah. Under Bill's guidance and parameters, Eli has been incorporating his personality into the menu.

Bill has countless awards and accolades to hang his hat on and an endless stream of respect from his peers. Being bad never looked so good.

ARUGULA SALAD WITH POTATOES, CREMINI MUSHROOMS & PANCETTA VINAIGRETTE

SERVES 4

For the pancetta vinaigrette (Yields 1 cup):

¼ cup rice vinegar

¼ cup red wine vinegar

¼ cup balsamic vinegar

½ cup diced pancetta, fat rendered and reserved

1 shallot, minced

2 tablespoons fresh thyme leaves

Zest and juice of 2 lemons

1 tablespoon sugar

1½ cups olive oil (or rendered pancetta fat)

½ cup extra-virgin olive oil

Salt and pepper to taste

For the arugula salad:

¼ cup fried small-diced potatoes

½ cup quartered cremini mushrooms,
    sautéed in pancetta fat used for dressing

¼ cup rendered pancetta, diced

½ pound fresh arugula

Salt and pepper to taste

6 tablespoons pancetta vinaigrette

8 ounces fresh goat cheese, crumbled

Special equipment:

Blender

To make the pancetta vinaigrette: Combine rice vinegar, red wine vinegar, balsamic vinegar, pancetta, shallot, thyme, lemon zest and juice, and sugar in a blender. Set pancetta fat and olive oil aside. Start the blender and slowly drizzle in olive oil and pancetta fat to emulsify. Season to taste with salt and pepper.

Extra dressing can be kept for a week. Rewarm in the microwave or by gently reheating on the stove.

To make the arugula salad: Warm the potatoes, mushrooms, and pancetta in a sauté pan. Place the arugula in a large bowl and season with salt and pepper. Drizzle in 6 tablespoons of warm pancetta vinaigrette and lightly toss the arugula to dress it evenly. Plate the salad and garnish with the potatoes, mushrooms, and pancetta. Top with the crumbled goat cheese.

PORK CHOPS WITH ROASTED BUTTERNUT SQUASH RISOTTO, GARLIC CREAM & CRISPY LEEKS

SERVES 4

For the veal stock (Yields 6 quarts of stock, 1 cup of demi-glace):

10 pounds veal marrow bones
2 onions, diced
2 carrots, peeled and diced
¼ bunch celery, diced
1 bunch parsley stems
1 bunch thyme stems
2 garlic heads, sliced crossways
1 bay leaf
8 whole black peppercorns
1 (10-ounce) can tomato puree

For the veal jus:

Prepared veal stock
½ cup red wine

For the roasted garlic cream:

2 heads garlic
1 cup olive oil
1 cup heavy cream
1 tablespoon chopped fresh thyme

For the greens:

1 pound greens (mustards, kale, collards, dandelion, endives, or a mixture)
2 tablespoons olive oil
2–3 garlic cloves, peeled and sliced
Ground black pepper to taste

For the leeks:

2 leeks
Oil for frying
Salt to taste

For the butternut squash risotto:

3 tablespoons unsalted butter, divided
2 tablespoons olive oil
¼ cup minced yellow onion
1 cup arborio rice
1½ quarts chicken stock, brought to a boil and kept hot
½ cup diced and roasted butternut squash
2 tablespoons grated Parmesan cheese
Pinch of chopped parsley
Salt and pepper to taste

For the pork chops:

4 (12-ounce) pork loin chops
2–4 tablespoons olive oil
Salt and pepper to taste

Special equipment:

Fine-mesh strainer
Blender or food processor
Deep fryer (optional)

To prepare the veal stock: Preheat oven to 350°F.

Place the bones in a large ovenproof pan and roast them until well browned, about 45 minutes to an hour; do not burn the bones. Add onions, carrots, and celery to browned bones. When all are browned, after about half an hour, place bones, vegetables, and remaining ingredients in a medium stockpot and cover with cold water. Bring to a boil, skim, and reduce to a simmer. Simmer for at least 6 to 8 hours, strain, and cool.

To prepare the veal jus: Place veal stock in a straight-sided pot that accommodates it with about an inch to spare. Place on a burner and bring to a boil. As stock comes to a boil, skim off the fat and foam. Reduce to a low boil. As soon as the stock has reduced enough to fit into a smaller straight-sided pot, strain through a fine-mesh strainer. As soon as it comes back to a boil, skim scrupulously. Repeat procedure until stock becomes thick. When near sauce consistency, add red wine and continue reducing.

To prepare the roasted garlic cream: Break the heads of garlic into individual cloves, leaving the cloves unpeeled. Place the cloves in a heavy pot and cover with the oil. Bring to a simmer over low to medium heat. (Caution: Garlic cloves can pop if heated too quickly!) When oil begins to bubble, reduce heat and allow the garlic to cook for 2 minutes.

Remove the pan from the heat and allow the mixture to cool. Strain the garlic through a fine-mesh strainer. When cooled, gently peel cloves and place them in a strainer and strain again. In a nonreactive pot, reduce the cream by one-fourth over low heat. Add drained garlic cloves and bring the mixture back to a simmer. Remove from heat and puree. Stir in the chopped thyme.

To prepare the greens: Stem, chop, and wash greens. Drain well. Heat olive oil in pan. Add garlic and cook until white. Add greens and cook until wilted. Season with pepper as necessary.

To prepare the crispy leeks: Julienne the white and light green parts of the leeks very finely. Wash and dry well. Heat oil in a heavy skillet or deep fryer to 350°F. Fry leeks in small batches until light brown. Lift out with a slotted spoon or round strainer and place on paper towels to drain. Season with a tiny bit of salt immediately after frying.

To prepare the butternut squash risotto: Heat butter and oil in a wide, heavy pot over low heat. Sweat onions until soft. Add rice and cook, stirring to coat the grains with butter, until opaque, about 3 to 5 minutes. Add ½ cup hot stock and stir until liquid is absorbed. Be careful to stir regularly so the risotto does not scorch. Continue adding stock in this fashion until rice is cooked al dente. Risotto should be a little loose, not soupy. Add squash, butter, cheese, and parsley. Adjust salt and pepper to taste.

To prepare the pork chops: If grilling, lightly rub the chops with oil, season with salt and pepper, and grill to desired doneness. If pan roasting, season them with salt and pepper. Heat the heavy skillet over high heat and add oil. Place chops in skillet. When well browned on the first side, turn and brown until ready on the second side. Place pan in 425°F oven and cook to desired temperature, at least 145°F.

To serve: Place a scoop of risotto on a plate and a portion of greens next to it. Set a finished chop atop the greens and risotto, drizzle garlic cream, nappe (or coat) with the veal jus, and top with crispy leeks.

Note from the chef: Prepare sauces and greens ahead of time; sauces can be made the day before. Have risotto in progress when you begin to cook the chops.

CHOCOLATE BREAD PUDDING

SERVES 4–6

2 loaves stale bread (preferably ciabatta)
1 pint heavy cream
1 pint half-and-half
1 vanilla bean, split and scraped
12 egg yolks
¾ cup granulated sugar
2 cups bittersweet chocolate chunks
2 cups fresh raspberries
Confectioners' sugar, for dusting

Special equipment:

Fine-mesh strainer
Round ramekins

Preheat oven to 325°F.

Dice loaves of bread into cubes and place them in a large bowl.

Bring cream, half-and-half, and vanilla bean to a boil. Mix yolks and sugar together just before the mixture comes to a boil. Temper the yolks with cream. Strain through a fine-mesh strainer. Pour over the bread cubes in bowl. Allow to soak for a few minutes. Toss in chocolate chunks and raspberries. Stir gently.

Ladle the mixture into round, greased ramekins. Bake for approximately 20 minutes or until set, turning regularly.

To serve: Dust with confectioners' sugar.

The Crested Duck Deli & Butcher Shop

1603 Broadway Avenue
Pittsburgh, PA 15216
(412) 892-9983
crestedduck.com

The Crested Duck isn't your traditional butcher shop. Here Executive Chef Kevin Costa does things a bit twisted. He uses locally sourced proteins, such as elk from a small farm in Saxonburg, rabbit, goat, and—of course—duck to make a variety of charcuterie in small batches.

Take one of his off-the-wall variations of salami: the Cannonball Salami. This dry-aged meat is made from all pork and flavored with vegetable ash made from leeks, natural sea salt infused with charcoal, and a smoky Lapsang souchong tea, which Kevin says, "smells like a campfire." And like its name suggests, the salami is shaped and aged in the form of a sphere, similar to a cannonball.

The Crested Duck's products can be found in many restaurants throughout the city, including Meat & Potatoes (page 115), Point Brugge Café (page 148), Legume (page 111), and E2 (page 58), and are sold at The Pittsburgh Public Market (pittsburghpublicmarket.org).

To create a charcuterie plate like a pro at home for yourself or a few dinner guests, Kevin offers of some of his tips for assembling the perfect plate:

MEAT

Variety is key! Pick two to three mildly seasoned items and one with a bold flavor profile.

- Cured meats: Pick something lean, like bresaola, and something fatty, such as coppa.
- Cured salami: Most salami have similar fat content, so choose a few based upon diameter and/or texture (i.e., dense/soft).
- Something cooked, such as fresh sausage or pâté.
- Smoked meat.

CHEESE

Think outside the box! Try a good mix of cow, goat, sheep, and blended cheeses. Pick cheeses of different textures (soft, semisoft, firm, and blue).

ACCOUTREMENTS

These are so important! Kevin suggests pairing something high in acid to offset the richness of the meat. He always picks cornichons, but other pickles and a strong, bold mustard work well, too. In addition, pair something sweet, such as dried fruit, fresh fruit in season, or quince paste, to offset the saltiness of the meats.

Christmas Lima Beans

French Camargue Rice
French red rice is from southwestern France. It has a rich beautiful color and excellent flavor, with subtle earthy. Makes a subtle early.

Dapple Grey Beans
This heirloom bean has a nice dense texture and beautiful spotted appearance. It pairs well with tomatoes and is thus well suited for chili.

5.25/LB

Black Beluga Lentils
The smallest of the lentil family.

Wehani Rice
Derived from Indian Basmati rice stock, this rice has a rich aroma of toasted peanuts when cooked and turns an earthy and ochre tint.

$ 4.00 LB

Red Quinoa Grain
A complete protein grain, high in lysine, iron, phosphorous, vitamins A, E and D. This nutritive grain is a great substitute for bulgar. It also makes a hearty, but light breakfast cereal.

$ 11

Chia Seeds

Appaloosa Beans

GOLDEN COMET
CORNISH ROCK

JAROSINSKI FARM - 31

CURE

5336 BUTLER STREET
PITTSBURGH, PA 15201
(412) 252-2595
CUREPITTSBURGH.COM
CHEF/OWNER: JUSTIN SEVERINO

For Ohio boy Justin Severino, the last decade has been a wild ride. From his Italian dinners with dad to traveling cross country and exploring the flavors of Northern California, Justin has had an incredible journey. It's been filled with deep insight into the practices and processes that are used to feed the hungry masses. It's also been filled with a personal mission to introduce healthier, more ethical, and more sustainable practices and processes to anyone who will listen.

Something that began as an act of searching for the truth in the food we eat has become a cure for an entire city in, well, Cure: a pride of the Pittsburgh food scene, situated in the Upper Lawrenceville neighborhood on the corner of cutting edge and back to basics.

The things Justin has seen and done, the things he's learned over the years are practically seeping out of his pores. One look at him or one probing question garners an outpouring of genuine passion and patient explanation. He's become well known across the United States for his honest approach to food preparation, and the best thing about him is his willingness—no, his need—to share that approach with everyone.

Cure is a multifaceted restaurant. It is one part cozy lodge with rustic wooden tables that go for miles, one part Mediterranean charcuterie, one part workshop, and one part classroom. It's all parts heart, from its chef and owner, to its staff and its thoughtfully prepared and presented dishes.

Sourcing seasonally from local farms, Justin's self-taught butchering ways allow for plates of hanger and rib eye steaks, smoked meats and fishes, and delicacies like bone marrow and foie gras to be served up the way they were meant to be. Ingredients are treated with care and are incorporated into his creations as naturally as possible as not to ruin the integrity of the taste or nutrition.

To understand and respect where your food is coming from will give you cause to enjoy a meal to its fullest potential. That mind-set is clear when you step foot into Cure and as you savor each bite of anything Justin creates.

PÂTÉ CICCIOLI

ITALIAN-STYLE COUNTRY PORK PÂTÉ

MAKES ONE 4 X 12 TERRINE MOLD; SERVES 12–15

3½ pounds pork shoulder or Boston butt, roughly cut into 1-inch dice

1 pound pork fatback, cut into 1-inch dice

2 tablespoons red wine vinegar

2 tablespoons salt, plus more to taste

1½ tablespoons whole black peppercorns

2 bay leaves

½ teaspoon chopped fresh thyme

2 cups pork or other meat stock

Salt and pepper to taste

Gourmet pickles (cornichons, red onion, cauliflower, and olives)

Gourmet mustards

Special equipment:

Parchment or waxed paper

4 x 12-inch Terrine mold

Palette knife

Place pork shoulder or Boston butt, pork fatback, red wine vinegar, salt, whole black peppercorns, bay leaves, and fresh thyme in a heavy-bottomed stockpot. Mix all ingredients thoroughly, making sure the salt is evenly distributed in the mixture. Cover and refrigerate overnight.

Remove the stockpot from the refrigerator and place on the stove top. Add stock. Cover with parchment or waxed paper, which should touch the meat mixture. Simmer over the lowest heat possible until the fat is translucent, about 3½ hours. Cool to room temperature.

When cooled, mix together with your hands, breaking the large pieces into smaller ones, until well combined. Taste for seasoning. Place into a terrine mold, lined with parchment or waxed paper. Pack layers as tight as possible. Cover the pâté and weight it with either another terrine mold or a heavy object like a box of salt wrapped in plastic wrap. Place in fridge overnight or until the mixture is cold in the center.

With a palette knife, gently remove the pâté from the terrine. Slice and plate the pâté with a variety of gourmet pickles and mustards.

Bone Marrow Ravioli with Bacon, Honey Mushrooms, Cava, Hazelnut, Wheatgrass & Sunchoke

MAKES 16–20 (2-INCH) RAVIOLI

This dish is incredibly rich and is meant to be consumed in small portions.

For the emulsified bone marrow (see note):

40 pounds veal marrow bones
18 gallons water, divided into two 9-gallon portions
4 pounds mirepoix (celery, carrots, and onion)

For the ravioli filling:

1 cup grated Parmesan cheese
2 cups emulsified bone marrow (see above)
Salt to taste

For the ravioli dough:

250 grams semolina flour
1 teaspoon salt
9 egg yolks
1 whole egg
1 tablespoon olive oil

For the wheatgrass sauce:

2 cups fresh, raw wheatgrass (found online and at
    health food or ethnic food stores)
1 teaspoon finely grated lemon zest
3 tablespoons hazelnut oil
5 grams soy lecithin
Salt to taste

For the sunchoke puree:

1 pound sunchokes (Jerusalem artichokes),
    washed and thinly sliced
¾ cup whole milk
2 tablespoons butter
Salt to taste

For assembling ravioli and for serving:

1 egg mixed with 2 tablespoons water
Flour
¼ pound bacon, diced
1 pound honey mushrooms, cleaned and ready to cook
1 gallon salted boiling water for cooking the ravioli
2 tablespoons emulsified bone marrow (see above)
2 tablespoons butter
2 tablespoons grated Parmesan cheese
6 tablespoons hazelnuts, toasted and chopped
Salt and pepper to taste
4 ounces cava (Taleggio cheese made from goat's milk)
Chervil, for garnish

Special equipment:

Metric kitchen scale
Chinois
Thermometer
Blender
Pastry bag
Food processor or stand mixer with dough hook
Pasta roller
Ravioli press
Pastry brush
Rolling pin
Immersion mixer

To prepare the emulsified bone marrow: Place marrow bones in a large container. Cover with 9 gallons of water and let soak overnight in the refrigerator.

After bones have soaked overnight, place the entire container, still filled with soaking water, in a large sink. Add more cold water into the container until the water runs clear. Drain and remove the bones from the container, and then place into a large stockpot with the mirepoix and 9 gallons of cold water.

Over medium heat, bring the pot to a simmer. Skim all the frothy impurities from the top during the simmering process. (Leave all the fat and rendered bone marrow in the pot.) Allow the stock to simmer for 8 hours. Strain the stock and the rendered bone marrow through a chinois into another stockpot. At high heat, rapidly reduce the stock and bone marrow mixture. As the stock reduces, lower the heat. The stock will be brown in color, thick, and glossy. Due to the protein in the stock and the friction caused by the boiling, the marrow and fat will become emulsified with the stock reduction. The end product should resemble caramel and yield about 3 quarts.

To prepare the ravioli filling: Preheat oven to 140°F.

Place the Parmesan cheese on a sheet tray and set it in a warm location.

Warm the emulsified bone marrow to 140°F. Place half the bone marrow in a blender with half the Parmesan cheese and puree on high until smooth. Repeat the process with the remaining bone marrow and Parmesan. Salt to taste and place in pastry bag. Store in a warm place while making the ravioli dough.

To prepare ravioli dough: Place flour and salt in a food processor or stand mixer with a dough hook. Combine egg yolks, 1 whole egg, and olive oil in a bowl, then slowly add to the dry ingredients and mix until smooth dough forms. Wrap dough in plastic and allow to rest for 1 hour at room temperature before rolling.

To assemble ravioli: Using a standard pasta machine, roll the pasta to the #7 setting. Cut the dough into 6-inch-long sheets. Stack the sheets, dusting each with a little flour, and cover the stack with a kitchen towel. Using a standard 12 x 4¼-inch, 12 (2-inch square) ravioli press, place a sheet of pasta on the mold, and make indentations with the press. Beat together 1 egg and 2 tablespoons water and brush this egg wash over the whole sheet.

Using a pastry bag, pipe the warm ravioli filling into the indentations, about 2 to 3 tablespoons of filling in each. Place another sheet of pasta on the top. Use a rolling pin to score and seal the ravioli. Place onto a tray dusted with semolina flour and store in the refrigerator.

To prepare the wheatgrass sauce: In a blender combine wheatgrass, lemon zest, and hazelnut oil and blend on low. Add soy lecithin. Blend on high to dissolve. Season with salt. Strain through chinois into a small saucepan and place in refrigerator until needed.

To prepare the sunchoke puree: Place sunchokes and milk into a medium-size saucepan. Cover with cartouche. Simmer at low heat until tender. Puree sunchokes with milk and butter until smooth. Season with salt.

To prepare for serving: In a large sauté pan render the bacon until crispy. Drain off half the fat. Add mushrooms. When the mushrooms are three-quarters cooked, place the ravioli into the boiling water. When the pasta is tender, drain it, reserving about ½ cup of the water, and add the ravioli to the pan of bacon and mushrooms along with the reserved pasta-cooking water. Bring to a simmer and add the emulsified bone marrow, butter, Parmesan cheese, and hazelnuts. Stir gently until you have a creamy sauce. Season with salt and pepper.

To serve: Place a spoonful of sunchoke puree in the center of the plate. Place ravioli atop the puree. Arrange some mushrooms over and around the ravioli. Place 3 to 5 torn chunks of cava on the plate and garnish with a few sprigs of chervil. Quickly warm the wheatgrass sauce and froth it with an immersion mixer. Dollop the froth on top and serve.

Note from the chef: Prepare emulsified bone marrow 48 hours prior to making and serving the ravioli.

Dinette

5996 Penn Circle South
Pittsburgh, PA 15206
(412) 362-0202
dinette-pgh.com
Chef/Owner: Sonja Finn

Sonja Finn's love of pizza began at a young age—six to be exact. It all started on a family trip to Italy. That's where she first experienced the joy of selecting her favorite toppings and then not sharing her creation with her older brother. The bond was instant, and her lifelong friendship with pizza was born.

That love still continues today in the form of her restaurant, Dinette.

Sonja opened Dinette in East Liberty during the beginning of its revitalization in 2008. She initially considered opening a sandwich shop but decided on pizza because, well, it's delicious. She also liked the challenge pizza presented. "Pizza is like a one-pot dish, but laid out on a crust. It's a challenge to put everything together and have people taste each individual flavor," says Sonja.

The pizza menu features classic flavor combinations that slightly push the envelope by highlighting seasonal ingredients. Much of the produce she uses comes from the rooftop garden planted by her father, Seth. Tomatoes, arugula, shishito peppers, figs,

lemon cucumbers, and herbs are all regularly featured on the menu, especially during the summer months.

One of Dinette's best-selling pizzas is the prosciutto pizza with arugula (from the garden, making it "twice as good," Sonja notes), Parmigiano Reggiano, fresh mozzarella, and tomato sauce. Other favorites include the pepperoni pizza and the salt-cured anchovy pizza, with jalapeños, capers, and fresh mozzarella.

The menu also features several seasonal salads and small starter plates. And if you have room for dessert, get the rice pudding. You won't be sorry. Often topped with seasonal fruit like figs or berries, this dessert is just sweet enough to be the perfect end to your meal.

TOMATO-FENNEL SOUP

SERVES 6–8

2 heads fennel
1 large yellow onion, peeled
1 teaspoon crushed red pepper flakes
3 tablespoons extra-virgin olive oil
2 (32-ounce) cans plum tomatoes
¼ cup heavy cream
Salt to taste
Parmigiano Reggiano to taste

Special equipment:

Blender
Fine-mesh strainer

Cut off fennel fronds (keep one piece for garnish). Cut fennel bulbs and onion into 1-inch pieces.

In a stockpot, sweat the fennel, onion, and red pepper flakes in the olive oil until translucent. Add water to barely cover the ingredients and let boil about 30 minutes to soften the fennel. Crush tomatoes with your hands and add them to the pot. Cook tomatoes until heated through. The sugars in the fennel and tomatoes can burn easily, so stir constantly and maintain medium heat.

Once the soup is done, puree it in batches in a blender and then push it through a fine-mesh strainer. Put the soup into a clean soup pot and bring it to a boil. Add cream and salt to taste. Adjust with water to achieve the desired consistency.

To serve: Top with Parmigiano Reggiano and fennel fronds.

GRILLED ROMAINE SALAD

SERVES 6

3 romaine hearts
⅔ cup extra-virgin olive oil
⅓ cup Champagne vinegar
¼ teaspoon salt, plus additional to taste
2 avocados, peeled, pitted, and thinly sliced
4 scallions, cleaned and thinly sliced on the bias
3 ounces ricotta salata
¼ cup saba (a sweet vinegar made from grapes)

Special equipment:

Grill or grill plate
Box grater

Cut the romaine hearts lengthwise into quarters through the core; the core will hold the leaves together. Mix olive oil and Champagne vinegar and about ¼ teaspoon salt to make a simple Champagne vinaigrette. Put half the romaine hearts into a bowl and sprinkle with 6 tablespoons of vinaigrette and a couple pinches of salt. Mix gently with your hands to prevent breaking up the romaine quarters. Coat well and ensure that the vinaigrette is incorporated into the leaves. Shake gently to prevent dripping, which could cause the grill to flare.

Place romaine pieces cut side down on a hot grill. Repeat with the second batch of romaine. After a couple minutes, when you have achieved good grill marks, turn romaine over and cook for another couple of minutes.

To serve: Place two romaine quarters on each plate. If romaine looks dry, drizzle it with remaining vinaigrette. Lay avocado slices on top, followed by scallions. Using a box grater shave ricotta salata on top. Drizzle saba over the salads.

Dish Osteria and Bar

128 South 17th Street
Pittsburgh, PA 15203
(412) 390-2012
DISHOSTERIA.COM
EXECUTIVE CHEF/OWNER: MICHELE SAVOIA

Nestled in Pittsburgh's Historic South Side neighborhood, on the corner of 17th and Sarah, sits Dish Osteria and Bar. The building had been a saloon since the late 1880s. While the space looks a bit different now than it did back in good old 1885, remnants of the past can be found all around. Tin walls and ceiling mesh beautifully with a copper bar top, exposed brick, and handmade tables and bar. One modern amenity remains absent from the decor: a TV.

Owner and Executive Chef Michele Savoia hails from Sicily and has spent a great deal of time in New York City. Upon moving to the 'Burgh, he instantly knew he'd feel at home in the South Side as it was the closest thing to The Village that he'd seen. Dish Osteria has been in operation since 2000. And since then, Michele has grown Dish from

a simple bar with a few small plates to a full-service Italian restaurant.

On opening day, Michele recalls just putting up a sign on the door that said he was open for business and waiting to see what would happen. Locals began pouring in and the place has been packed ever since.

Thanks to all of the great local farmers and purveyors, the offerings at Dish include the freshest of ingredients and include pan-fried eggplant (you won't find a fryer anywhere in the joint), seafood pasta, and beef carpaccio, plus salads and antipastos. On the dessert menu, limoncello cheesecake, chocolate bread pudding, and tiramisu (made with imported mascarpone cheese) are all prepared by Michele's mother-in-law!

Since there's no TV, guests are invited to peruse the extensive wine list, select a glass or bottle, and sit back to enjoy a phenomenal meal with the soft flicker of candlelight bouncing off the walls as music and laughter fill the air.

Spaghetti al Sugo di Seppie

Spaghetti with Fresh Cuttlefish

SERVES 4

4 medium size fresh cuttlefish, cleaned
   (Ink sac removed and reserved)
Olive oil for cooking
1 small onion, sliced thin
1 small garlic bulb, sliced
1 teaspoon crushed red pepper
Salt and pepper to taste
1 cup fresh parsley, minced
½ cup white wine
10 tablespoons tomato paste
Water as necessary
4 servings cooked spaghetti pasta of your choice

Clean cuttlefish by removing skin. Separate tentacles and set aside. Remove eyes and interiors and discard. Cut the skinless tube in thin strips. (Or have your local fishmonger prepare the fish for you!)

In a 3-inch deep sauté pan put olive oil, onion, and garlic. Sauté over medium-low heat until onion and garlic are slightly golden. Then add crushed red pepper. Increase cooking temperature to medium and add tentacles once onions and garlic are golden. Stir frequently.

When tentacles turn a reddish color, add in the cut tube strips. Season with salt and pepper to taste. Add half of the parsley and white wine. Continue cooking over medium heat for 3 to 5 minutes and then add tomato paste. Stir, while adding small amounts of water at the time until the sauce reaches a creamy consistency. (Not too thick, not too runny.)

Taste for seasoning and then add the ink sacs you reserved. With a wooden spoon break them into the sauce, which should become black. Add the rest of the parsley and serve tossed with spaghetti.

E2

5904 BRYANT STREET
PITTSBURGH, PA 15206
(412) 441-1200
E2PGH.COM
CHEF/OWNER: KATE ROMANE

Winter storms are usually bad for business. That is, unless you're E2 (pronounced "*E* squared") in Highland Park. The quaint twenty-eight-seat Italian restaurant opened its doors for the first time during one of Pittsburgh's biggest snowstorms. "Snowmageddon" was a grade-schoolers dream and officially shut down the city for almost four days in February 2010. "The power was out. The roads weren't plowed. And people were just walking around in Highland Park," says Kate Romane, chef and owner of E2. "So we put out a hand-painted HOT SOUP sign, sent out an e-mail to the neighborhood, and sold out of food in an hour."

After that, E2 was officially a part of the community.

Kate moved to Pittsburgh in 1997 and quickly became submerged in food while living and working at an Italian bakery in the Strip District. "All these old Italian guys started to

teach me the small stuff: how to make a red sauce, how to make bread. I just really got turned on to food and ended up going to culinary school." After culinary school, Kate took on catering and even had the opportunity to cook for President Obama while he was in town for the 2009 G-20 summit. It was during her catering days that she found the space for what would become E2.

Open for dinner and brunch, both menus are simple and dictated by neighborhood taste buds and local farmers. You'll find ample amounts of greens and tomatoes in the warmer months and plenty of hearty root veggies during the winter. But let's not forget that E2 is Italian to the core, so you'll always find a variety of pasta dishes and, of course, spaghetti and meatballs.

To help fight off hunger pangs or to ease a hangover, Kate introduced OMGs (Oh My Gosh, I'm so hungry) during brunch. Homemade doughnuts, beignets, and *zeppole* (fried dough with pepper, Parmesan, and optional anchovies) make waking up just a little easier. If that doesn't do the trick, a chalkboard menu full of varieties of polenta, frittata, omelettes, hash, and salads surely will.

ANTIPASTO

SERVES 1 SMALL PARTY

For the Gorgonzola mess:

4 cups crumbled mild blue cheese
¾ cup fresh basil leaves
1 tablespoon red wine vinegar
2 tablespoons Sriracha hot sauce

For the sweet peppers with roasted garlic:

2 red peppers, seeded and cut to finger size
2 cloves garlic, peeled and sliced
Olive oil
Salt and pepper to taste

For the caraway onions:

4 onions, peeled and julienned
Olive oil
3 tablespoons caraway seeds
3 tablespoons salt
6 ounces can cola (½ can)
2 tablespoons balsamic vinegar

For the white anchovies with parsley and celery:

1 cup marinated white anchovies
1 stalk celery, sliced super thin on the bias
½ cup roughly chopped flat-leaf parsley
½ lemon, cut in small wedges
Olive oil

For the roasted baby parsnips and baby carrots with thyme and sea salt:

2 cups quartered baby parsnips
2 cups quartered baby carrots
Olive oil
1 tablespoon dried fennel seed
Sea salt and pepper to taste
2 sprigs fresh thyme, leaves pulled from the stem

Bread, olive oil, and prosciutto, for serving

Special equipment: Food processor

To prepare the Gorgonzola mess: **Add blue cheese, basil leaves, red wine vinegar, and Sriracha into a food processor and mix until smooth.**

To prepare the sweet peppers with roasted garlic: **In a saucepan, sauté red peppers, garlic, olive oil, and salt and pepper to taste over medium heat until soft. Serve warm or at room temperature.**

To prepare the caraway onions: **In a saucepan over low heat, sweat onions with olive oil, caraway seeds, and salt down to a golden brown. Add cola and balsamic vinegar. Sauté until the onions are a rich caramel color. The caraway onions can be eaten by themselves or on a sandwich.**

To prepare the white anchovies with parsley and celery: **In a bowl, toss marinated anchovies, celery, flat-leaf parsley, and lemon wedges. Drizzle with olive oil.**

To prepare the roasted baby parsnips and baby carrots with thyme and sea salt: **Preheat oven to 375°F. Toss parsnips and carrots in olive oil, fennel seed, and sea salt and pepper. Evenly spread parsnips and carrots on a sheet tray. Roast vegetables in the oven until soft, but still have a crunch, approximately 7 to 8 minutes. While still warm, garnish with fresh thyme.**

To serve: **Pair with a nice loaf of bread, good olive oil, and prosciutto, if available, for a colorful spread.**

Note from the chef: **Antipasto can be made a day or two ahead.**

Churchview Farm

3897 Churchview Avenue
Pittsburgh, PA 15236
(412) 496-5623
churchviewfarmpgh.com

You could say soil runs through Tara Rockacy's veins. She's a third-generation farmer who respects tradition and the ecosystem. She also happens to be the partner of Kate Romane, chef and owner of E2 (page 58) in Highland Park.

In addition to E2, Churchview Farm provides Dish Osteria (page 56), The Crested Duck Deli & Butcher Shop (page 44), and several other Pittsburgh establishments with chemical-free produce year-round. Heirloom tomatoes (forty-seven or so varieties) plus other fruits and vegetables, raw and unfiltered honey from seven hives, and eggs from about ten different heritage breeds of chickens are all available through Churchview Farm.

To experience the local goodness yourself, you can visit or volunteer at the farm, join the community-supported agriculture (CSA) program, or pick up some produce during a local farmers' market.

Eat Unique

305 South Craig Street
Pittsburgh, PA 15213
(412) 683-9993
EATUNIQUECAFE.COM
Owners: Dave and Lisa Brown

Sandwiches, soups, and salads can often be boring to eat. But Eat Unique electrifies your taste buds with tasty combinations of fresh ingredients. Imagine a spicy grilled cheese and bacon sandwich paired with a bowl of white turkey chili. Or a meatloaf melt sandwich with blue cheese and barbecue sauce served with a Sea Salt Chocolate Chip Cookie for dessert (cue: mouth watering).

Owner Lisa and her husband, Dave, opened Eat Unique in Oakland in 1997 in the former location of Buns & Udders, a bakery and ice cream shop. Originally the couple opened the space as a coffee shop called Craig Street Coffee. After introducing some well-received homemade soups and sandwiches, they knew they were onto something big. The name change to Eat Unique came about ten years later when they transformed the business into a cafe and catering operation. "We are inventive about our ingredients and what ingredients we put together," says Lisa. "And when the name was suggested to us, it just clicked."

The most popular items on their ever-changing menu include impressive sandwiches and scratch-made soups. "My one true talent in the world is the sandwiches I come up with," says Lisa jokingly. One of the all-time most popular sandwiches that Lisa has created is the Summer Sandwich: focaccia bread, pesto, ripe tomatoes, fresh mozzarella, roasted red peppers, onions, and spring greens. But she doesn't take all of the credit for coming up with these tasty combinations; she gives much praise to her kitchen staff.

One of the best complements to any salad, soup, or sandwich is dessert. And Eat Unique cranks out some mighty fine cookies and sweet treats, such as the Sea Salt Chocolate Chip Cookies, a perfect combination of sweet, salty, and ooey-gooey.

Sea Salt Chocolate Chip Cookies

MAKES 30–36 COOKIES

3½ cups all-purpose flour

1 teaspoon baking soda

1½ teaspoons coarse ground sea salt

½ pound (2 sticks) salted butter (no substitutes)

¾ cup granulated sugar

¾ cup light brown sugar

2 large eggs

1 tablespoon vanilla extract

2 cups real chocolate chips

Special equipment:

Stand mixer with paddle attachment

Parchment paper

Preheat oven to 350°F.

Sift flour, baking soda, and sea salt into a bowl. Set aside. Using a stand mixer with a paddle attachment, cream butter and sugars together until light and fluffy and well incorporated. Add eggs one at a time, mixing well after each addition. Mix in vanilla. Reduce speed to low, add the dry ingredients, and mix until just combined, about 5 to 10 seconds. Add chocolate chips and mix to incorporate them.

Line a baking sheet with parchment paper. Scoop mounds of dough the size of generous golf balls onto the baking sheet.

Bake until golden brown but still soft, approximately 8 to 12 minutes. (Be sure to check after 8 minutes to make sure they do not overbake.) Remove from oven. Leave cookies on the baking sheet for 10 minutes before transferring to a wire rack to continue cooling.

Eat warm with a big glass of milk!

EDEN

735 COPELAND STREET
PITTSBURGH, PA 15232
(412) 802-7070
EDENPITT.COM
CHEF/OWNER: HILARY ZOZULA

Walk into Eden and walk into Chef/Owner Hilary Zozula's laboratory. The raw, vegan, and gluten-free menu items result from her experiments in the kitchen. "It is really more science than cooking," Hilary explains. "There are techniques you can follow for raw food, but you really just have to start playing and mixing textures and temperatures."

This culinary chemistry produces items not found elsewhere inside city limits, from creamy stuffed collard greens to raw, vegan foie gras (without a goose in sight). Organic, free-range chicken also makes menu appearances when available. The menu rotates every three months, allowing different, mostly from-scratch dishes to shine. The local art lining the walls also changes every six weeks, making the restaurant a veritable gallery for local artists to showcase their talents. From the decor to the fare, this cozy space on Copeland Street is a haven of creativity.

Hilary, self-taught in food creation, credits family for her inspiration. Raised following a raw, vegan diet in California, she gained an appreciation for healthy eating. "We could go outside of our front door and take an avocado from our avocado tree," she reminisces. "It was totally like a stereotypical hippie commune." While the Pittsburgh landscape doesn't provide for prime avocado picking, Hilary hopes that Eden emulates that experience of walking into a garden and bringing in fresh and healthy foods to the table.

The neighborhood has certainly taken notice, but some folks still are a little wary before trying the interesting menu offerings. Hilary understands their apprehension but knows that fear will subside once the forks meet their lips. "Eden isn't about being vegan or vegetarian. Eden is just about being healthy."

Cashew Cheese

MAKES 1 WHEEL

3 cups raw cashews
Juice of 2 lemons
2 tablespoons apple cider vinegar
1 tablespoon sea salt

Special equipment:

Food processor or blender
Food dehydrator with nonstick sheets

Dry blend the cashews into a coarse powder using a food processor or blender.

Mix the cashew powder, lemon juice, apple cider vinegar, and sea salt together. This mixture should form a thick paste.

Use your hands to form the paste into a round, flat disc. Place disk on a nonstick dehydrator sheet. Place in the dehydrator at 120°F for 12 hours.

Remove the sheet from the dehydrator and chill in the refrigerator for 6 hours before enjoying.

CHOCOLATE PECAN PIE WITH WALNUT CREAM
SERVES 6–8

For the crust:

1 cup dates
1 cup pecans
1 teaspoon sea salt

For the pie filling:

3 cups dates
1 cup coconut oil
1 cup cacao powder
1 cup pecans
1 teaspoon vanilla
¾ cup water

For the walnut cream:

½ cup walnuts
Handful of dates
⅔ cup water

Special equipment:

Food processor or blender
8-inch springform pan

To prepare the crust: Blend dates, pecans, and sea salt together using a food processor or blender until you achieve a coarse texture. Press the mixture into the bottom of a springform pan. Cover the entire bottom of the pan.

To make the pie filling: Use a high-speed blender to blend dates, coconut oil, cacao powder, pecans, vanilla, and water until smooth. The resulting mixture should be thick and have a silky texture. Pour the mixture into the springform pan, over the crust you have pressed into the bottom. Place the pie in the refrigerator for 12 hours.

The walnut cream can be made after the pie has set.

To make the walnut cream: Place the ingredients into a blender and blend until smooth. Drizzle the cream over the top of the chilled pie.

El Burro Comedor

1108 Federal Street
Pittsburgh, PA 15212
(412) 904-3451
ELBURROPGH.COM
OWNERS: DEREK BURNELL AND WES DERENOUARD

Pittsburgh is no Southern California. Snow in April kicks any kind of California dreaming to the curb.

Business partners and SoCal natives Derek Burnell, of Round Corner Cantina, and Wes DeRenouard unfortunately haven't brought the Cali sunshine to western Pennsylvania, but they have brought burritos, tacos, and other traditional flavors found along the border. OK, so no sunshine? No problem. One bite of this deliciousness on Federal Street will brighten any day.

The menu, painted in yellow and red on the back wall, offers standard taqueria fare. Tacos can be ordered hard or soft shell or rolled. The burritos, like chile relleno and shrimp diablo verde, are hearty, satisfying choices. Like meat, cheese, and everything that is good about life? Make sure to indulge in the *carne asada* fries: french fries topped with shredded meat, cheese, and guacamole.

Every menu item is made in-house, including the three hot sauces, salsa, guacamole, slow-cooked meats, and the daily, off-menu specials like vegan chorizo. The chips are even fried fresh each morning. "This is what I grew up eating," says Wes, a San Diego transplant.

El Burro has apparently been in the works for a while. Derek and Wes became friends in the second grade and fixed their eyes on the taco-shop prize. "Derek and I always talked about opening a taco shop since we met." Two decades and some change later, the boys found the perfect home in the Northside for their project and opened El Burro in 2012. "The community here is the best," says Wes. "They have really embraced the concept and made it easy for us to get started."

Take that chilly Pittsburgh—California dreams do come true.

SHREDDED BEEF TACOS

SERVES 8

2 poblano peppers

1 onion

2 tomatoes

2½ pounds chuck roast

3 cloves garlic

2 teaspoons paprika

1 teaspoon ground coriander

1 teaspoon ground cumin

Salt and pepper to taste

½ cup water

8 corn tortillas

Cilantro leaves, for garnish

Lime wedges, for serving

Preheat oven to 325°F.

Chop poblano peppers, peel and dice the onion, and peel tomatoes; leave the tomatoes whole. Save some of the diced onion for garnish.

Place the chuck roast, poblano peppers, onion, tomatoes, and garlic in a roasting pan. Add paprika, coriander, cumin, and a dash of salt and pepper. Add water. Roast in the oven for 2½ to 3 hours until meat is tender enough for shredding.

Drain roast, leaving vegetables and meat. Using a fork, shred the meat.

To serve: Warm the tortillas. Portion the meat onto tortillas. Garnish with diced onion and cilantro. Serve with a wedge of lime.

THE ENRICO BISCOTTI COMPANY

2022 PENN AVENUE
PITTSBURGH, PA 15222
(412) 281-2602
ENRICOBISCOTTI.COM
OWNER/CHEF: LARRY LAGATTUTA

It's 4 A.M. and while you're snuggled in bed, Larry Lagattuta is starting his day. Soon he'll be filling the brick oven at Enrico Biscotti in the Strip District with breads, cakes, pies, and pizza.

Like countless bakers before him, Larry grew up in the kitchen. He was taught the basics of preparing Italian favorites from his mother and grandmother. It wasn't until fifteen years into a career as an account executive that baking reentered his life. "I became really great friends with a baker from Tuscany. He had to make thirty pounds of pastry one night and couldn't do it himself. I went to his house, worked in his basement, and then sat on his back porch eating and drinking till the sun came up." That one serendipitous moment sent Larry down a new yet familiar path.

He opened the authentic Italian *pasticceria* (bakery) making what he knew best: his grandma's biscotti. The bakery has more than just biscotti now. Larry and his team crank out about 1,200 pounds of cookies a day. Award-winning macaroons, various Italian cookies, breads, and a few American-pastry standards like peanut butter cookies, pecan sandies, and brownies fill the display case.

The bakery also grew in size when he took over the auto mechanic's garage next door. There he put in his beloved brick oven, which has been continuously churning every day for twenty years, and started making bread. Bread evolved to soup, soup evolved to salad, and the cafe menu was born.

The approach at the cafe is simplicity. Bread is made with yeast, salt, flour, and water. Pasta puttanesca is made like it is in Sicily with spinach, one anchovy, and no tomato sauce. Pasta Alfredo is made with three ingredients: pasta water, Parmesan Reggiano, and pasta. "That's the thing about our food, it's simple," says Larry. And sometimes simple is all you need to start your day.

GROUND HAZELNUT RICOTTA CAKE

MAKES 1 (9-INCH) ROUND CAKE

½ pound (2 sticks) unsalted butter,
   cut into small pieces
1¼ cups granulated sugar
8 eggs
1 cup ricotta cheese
½ cup flour
1½ cups finely ground hazelnuts
½ pound semisweet chocolate, melted

Special equipment:

Stand mixer with paddle attachment
Double boiler

In a stand mixer with a paddle attachment, cream the butter and sugar. Add the eggs, one at a time until they are incorporated into the sugar mixture. Add ricotta, flour, and ground hazelnuts.

Preheat the oven to 350°F.

Pour the batter into a 9-inch round cake pan that has been greased and floured and bake about 40 minutes or until the cake is firm in the center.

Remove the cake from the oven and set aside to cool for 10 minutes. Run a knife around the edge of the pan and invert the pan to remove the cake.

In a double boiler, melt semisweet chocolate over medium heat. Pour the melted chocolate onto the center of the cake and spread it over the top of the cake until it is completely covered. Allow cake to cool until the chocolate is set.

Using a sharp knife that has been warmed in hot water, slice the cake and serve.

Biscotti Crumb Scallops with Basil Curry

SERVES 4

3 large almond biscotti

8 dry sea scallops

1 egg

2 tablespoons unsalted butter

½ cup heavy cream

2 tablespoons curry powder

Salt and pepper to taste

1 bunch basil, leaves removed

Special equipment:

Hand blender or food processor

Place the biscotti into a plastic bag. Using a rolling pin, crush the biscotti until they are very fine crumbs.

Pat the scallops dry. In a medium bowl, crack the egg and stir with a fork until beaten. Dip the scallops in the egg. Place scallops into plastic bag filled with biscotti crumbs. Shake the bag gently until the scallops are completely coated with biscotti crumbs.

In a medium-size skillet, heat 1 tablespoon butter. Sauté the scallops on medium heat for 1 minute on each side; the scallops should just begin to brown. Remove the scallops from the pan.

In a small saucepan, melt the remaining butter. After the butter is completely melted, add the heavy cream, curry powder, and salt and pepper to taste. Add the basil leaves to the cream mixture. Blend the cream mixture with a hand blender or process in a food processor until the basil blends into the cream mixture and turns it a light green color.

To serve: Spoon 3 tablespoons basil cream onto a plate. Place two scallops onto the plate. Serve at once.

FARM KINGS

FREEDOM FARMS
795 PITTSBURGH ROAD
BUTLER, PA 16002
(724) 586-5551
FREEDOMFARMSPA.COM

"Work can be fun; maintaining a family relationship is not easy, but it is worth it; and people should take pride in what they do."

Words to live by from Joe King, business manager of Freedom Farms in Butler County. Joe owns and operates the farm, founded in 2009, with two of his nine brothers, Pete and Tim. Their produce, chicken, beef, and pork can be found at farmers' markets throughout the 'Burgh as well as their home farm in Butler, and the Cafe and Carry Out in New Kensington. For the sweet tooth, the boys also operate Boldy's Homemade Goodies in Butler, specializing in fresh doughnuts daily.

Oh, and you know, these fellows just happen to be reality television stars. *Farm Kings,* on the Great American Country network, focuses on the blood, sweat, and tears of the King family business. No sparkle and glitter here. Honest American grit mixed with a loving family dynamic makes for a compelling story arc. The occasional shirtless Farm King doesn't hurt either. "We are big on farming," says Joe. "We want to make it fun and cool again."

The trio of young men, and their costar brother Dan, are certainly doing their part to make farming en vogue. Farming since birth (essentially), they will continue to do their part to supply the area with fresh foods. "Our goal is to feed a twenty-mile radius and be the best that we can be in this region," maintains Joe.

Hard work never takes a holiday, whether the cameras are on or off. But their love for farming brings the boys back to the fields day in and day out. Joe wouldn't have it any other way: "It isn't easy, there are no guarantees, but you just have to take a chance. I bounce out of bed every morning, and it has nothing to do with a paycheck."

Food Glorious Food

5906 Bryant Street
Pittsburgh, PA 15206
(412) 363-5330
FOODGLORIOUSFOODONLINE.ORG
Owners: Tom Hambor and Brad Walter

It was a secret. Posters on signposts would appear every Saturday announcing that Food Glorious Food had baked goods. The treats would sell out, and the posters would come down. It would behoove folks to be in the know about this process. "We really didn't tell anyone," says Tom Hambor, co-owner and pastry chef. "I don't even think we did a mailer."

Food Glorious Food opened up shop as a cooking school and gourmet gift shop in 2000. Owners Brad Walter and Tom had renovated a worn-out space on Bryant Street in Highland Park, complete with kitchen and storefront. After years of teaching culinary classes to individuals and at corporate retreats, they decided to give pastries the center stage—not a leap, as Tom spent his youth watching his mother make sweets. He honed his own baking craft in Ohio, in school at the University of Akron and working in

Cleveland's best restaurants. Starting a once-per-week "secret" bakery proved to be the perfect outlet for Tom's acquired tastes and skills.

Now the word is out. Food Glorious Food is open Tuesday through Saturday, offering baked goods, glorious baked goods. More than forty delectable sweet and savory options are on the menu. The bakery is known for its decadent White Lily Cake, a vanilla cake with fresh raspberries and whipped cream. Tom has spent decades tinkering with recipes to bring the confections as close to perfect as possible. The signature White Lily Cake succeeds because it has, according to Tom, "a mixture of all the little baking tricks I've learned in the past rolled into one."

While Pittsburgh is the perfect place to call home, Brad and Tom hold a special place in their hearts for Italy. They travel, typically once per year, to the boot-shaped country, making friends and finding the best dining locales. They invite customers to join them on their culinary journey on a ten-to-twelve-day tour, with cooking lessons and private dining experiences. While they know the places to go in Italy, Tom jokes about his mastery of the Italian language: "I know how to read the menu."

Tart Tatin

MAKES 1 (9-INCH) TART

Use fruit that is in season and make substitutions between apples, pears, plums, peaches, or apricots.

Flour for dusting

1 sheet puff pastry

6 medium-size apples or pears, *or* 1 dozen plums, peaches, or apricots

8 tablespoons (1 stick) unsalted butter

1 cup granulated cane sugar

Special equipment:

9-inch skillet

On a lightly floured work surface, place the sheet of puff pastry. Roll it into a 10-inch square and cut into a 10-inch round. Place on a baking sheet and set in the refrigerator.

Peel apples or pears, cut them into quarters, and slice out the cores. Peaches, plums, and apricots do not need peeling; halve and pit them.

Melt butter in an ovenproof 9-inch skillet over medium heat. Add sugar to the melted butter; the sugar should be evenly distributed on the bottom of the skillet. Arrange the fruit tightly on top of the sugar in a decorative pattern. All of the fruit will not fit, but as it cooks, there will be room to add more. Continue cooking, gently shaking the pan so the fruit doesn't stick. Cook for 20 to 30 minutes, or until the syrup turns a medium caramel color. Remove the skillet from the heat.

While the fruit cooks, preheat the oven to 400°F.

Cover the fruit with the chilled round of puff pastry. Tuck the pastry between the fruit and sides of the skillet.

Bake for 30 minutes until the puff pastry looks done and golden brown. Let the tart cool for 1 minute.

To serve: Carefully invert onto a serving platter, leaving the skillet upside down until all is released. If the tart does not release after a minute, flip back into the skillet and warm over a flame to release, and invert again.

Note from the chef: The tart is best served at room temperature the same day it is made.

Mozzarella Cheese Roulade

MAKES 20 CROSTINI

16 ounces mozzarella curd

1–2 teaspoons salt

Hot water, as needed

8–10 basil leaves

6 ounces roasted red peppers, drained

20 crostini slices

Olive oil for serving

Balsamic vinegar for serving

Salt for serving

Special equipment:

Thermometer

Chop the curd into ½-inch pieces and place it in a large bowl. Add salt and hot water (heated to about 180°F) so that the water reaches the top of the curd in the bowl. Stir gently for 2 to 3 minutes, allowing the curd to absorb the heat from the water. Drain and repeat with more hot water.

Stir the curd gently with a wooden spoon. Begin to gather the curd pieces into one area of the bowl to form a large ball. Remove the ball from the water. Stretch and knead to ensure that all of the curd has been cooked.

Place the curd back into the water to heat. Repeat this process until the curd looks like taffy.

Put the cheese on a clean work surface. Form into a rectangle, about 8 x 16 inches. Pat dry. Cover half with basil; cover the other half with red peppers.

Roll the cheese like a jelly roll. Wrap tightly with plastic wrap and place in an ice bath for 10 minutes. Once chilled, remove the plastic wrap.

To serve: Slice the cheese into ¼-inch medallions. Place on crostini slices and serve with drizzles of olive oil, balsamic vinegar, and salt.

FRANKTUARY

DOWNTOWN:
325 OLIVER AVENUE
PITTSBURGH, PA 15222

LAWRENCEVILLE:
3810 BUTLER STREET
PITTSBURGH, PA 15201
(412) 586-7224
FRANKTUARY.COM
OWNERS: MEGAN LINDSEY AND TIM TOBITSCH

The owners of Franktuary, Megan Lindsey and Tim Tobitsch, have been crafting rhetoric wit since the doors of their hot doggery opened in a church basement in Downtown Pittsburgh in 2004. Their empire now includes the original location, a traveling truck, and a bar/restaurant in Lawrenceville. The offerings have expanded, but their vocabulary has hit the ceiling. "All of the hot dog and religious puns we have left are borderline offensive," laughs Tim.

Megan and Tim became fast friends as freshmen at Grove City College in Grove City, Pennsylvania. The two played some mean brass in the marching band and also schemed to promote the school's roller hockey club, including some interesting choices for fan attire: "I once used the flame-resistant curtains from my dorm windows, which we weren't allowed to remove, as a robe for an Old Testament prophet costume," Megan reminisces. "It was one of my most ferocious acts of rebellion."

Upon graduation, the two joined forces again to start a restaurant. Tim grew up in New York, where he fostered a great appreciation for hot dogs. His love for this simple

dish became the perfect jumping-off point for the pair. "We decided to take something ordinary and use it as a base to introduce people to healthier food," says Tim.

Thus the hot dogs on this menu are not your standard encased meat. Take, for example, the Underdog, made with grass-fed beef sourced from a farm in New Zealand. Or, try the Locavore, sourced from local farms and produced in small batches. "You are eating something you like, but it is better for you and better for the environment," says Megan. With toppings choices like mango salsa, Thai peanut sauce, and a smooshed pierogi, these dogs are easy to love.

Despite being told that business with a buddy is not a good idea, Megan and Tim maintain a strong friendship. "You have to accept people for who they are in order to be successful," Tim observes. Can we get an "amen"?

GRASS-FED BEEF CHILI

SERVES 6–8

Franktuary loves local farmers, and grass-fed beef chili is a great way to showcase meat from animals that have been fed their natural diet—no corn, soybeans, or other questionable feed-lot goop—and have enjoyed their healthy, antibiotic-free lives outdoors on living pasture.

2 pounds grass-fed beef (preferably from a local farm)

2 stalks fresh celery

1 white or yellow onion

1 red or green pepper, seeded

3 teaspoons olive oil

2 (15-ounce) cans kidney beans, drained

1½ (15-ounce) cans white cannellini or great Northern beans, drained

1 (10-ounce) can diced tomatoes and green chiles (Rotel preferred)

1½ cups fresh salsa, hot or medium

1 (15-ounce) can diced tomatoes

1 (15-ounce) can pizza sauce without high-fructose corn syrup

1½ tablespoons minced fresh or canned jalapeños

2⅓ teaspoons minced fresh garlic

4 teaspoons dark chili powder

1½ teaspoons crushed red pepper flakes

2⅓ teaspoons ground cumin

Brown beef on medium heat—not too high—in a large pot. While the meat is browning, dice the celery, onion, and pepper. In a separate saucepan, cook the vegetables in olive oil until softened.

Once vegetables have lightly cooked, add to meat and stir to combine. Periodically break apart large chunks of beef while the mixture continues to cook.

In a separate bowl, combine kidney beans, white beans, diced tomatoes and green chiles, fresh salsa, canned diced tomatoes, pizza sauce, jalapeños, garlic, chili powder, crushed red pepper flakes, and cumin. Add this mixture to the pot of meat and vegetables. Simmer very gently for 1 hour.

Ginzer

MAKES 1 COCKTAIL

Franktuary's Ginzer combines a historic local spirit, distilled just a mile down the road, with sweet citrus and a bit of red-pepper heat. If you aren't lucky enough to live in our region and purchase Wigle Whiskey products, try Bols Genever or a high-quality gin like Hendrick's.

2 slices red pepper
2 ounces best-quality gin (Wigle Ginever preferred)
¾ ounce fresh-squeezed lime juice
¾ ounce simple syrup
5 dashes Sriracha hot sauce
1 cucumber
1 cup ice cubes

In a heavy cocktail shaker, muddle the slices of red pepper. Add the gin, lime juice, simple syrup, and Sriracha to the shaker. Shake all ingredients vigorously for 30 seconds. Double strain, using a Hawthorne strainer and a fine mesh strainer, into a rocks glass filled with ice.

Using a vegetable peeler, peel a ¾-inch section of the cucumber, starting at the top of the cucumber and peeling down to the bottom; discard. Slice again, getting half green peel and half white flesh on the cucumber strip.

Coil the two-toned cucumber strip around the inner rim of the glass. It should sit nicely on the top of the ice.

WIGLE WHISKEY

2401 SMALLMAN STREET
PITTSBURGH, PA 15222
(412) 224-2827
WIGLEWHISKEY.COM

"It was a conversation that got out of control," recalls Meredith Grelli, co-owner of Wigle Whiskey, about the distillery's founding. Wigle is all family: The owners include Meredith; her husband, Alex; her brother, Eric Meyer; and Meredith and Eric's parents, Mary Ellen and Mark Meyer. On a vacation to Canada, the crew visited small, family ice vineyards and loved the vibe. "We figured if Canadians can do it . . ." laughs Meredith. So the family went all in and brought whiskey distilling back to western Pennsylvania.

Wigle Whiskey, named after Phillip Wigle, a lead character in the Whiskey Rebellion of the late 1700s, distills organic white rye whiskey, organic white wheat whiskey, organic ginever (gin distilled from whiskey rather than the traditional vodka based gin), and honey-sweetened rum. Cask-aged whiskey and ginever can also be purchased on site, but batches run out fast. Aged whiskey can be achieved at home by purchasing a tiny barrel kit for the white spirits.

Wigle liquor is a hot sell in Pittsburgh and is featured at restaurants across town. (And you can cook up a cocktail at home—excitement! See Franktuary's Ginzer (facing page) and Tender's Van Buren on page 184. Oh, and how about some soup? Thin Man Sandwich Shop uses Wigle Rye Whiskey for the pumpkin soup on page 190). For more information on where to purchase these fine libations, or to find out how to take a swell tour of the facilities, visit Wigle's website.

FUKUDA

4770 LIBERTY AVENUE
PITTSBURGH, PA 15224
(412) 377-0916
FUKUDAPGH.COM
CHEF/OWNER: MATT KEMP
OWNER: HOON KIM

Who knows the correct way to eat sushi? If you're unsure, keep reading so Chef Matt Kemp can teach you a thing or two in case you've been doing it wrong all these years.

Matt, soft-spoken but well versed in culinary matters and all things raw fish, kindly explained exactly what to do with wasabi, when to use chopsticks, and that too much soy sauce ruins the experience and flavor of what you're meant to be eating.

Matt and co-owner Hoon Kim met while working together in Pittsburgh's historic Strip District. They bonded instantly and, knowing they aimed to increase the caliber of traditional Japanese food in our fair city, opened Fukuda in a small Bloomfield storefront. Over a matter of mere months, Fukuda, meaning "blessed rice paddy," went from the new kid in town to that place you've got to try. To garner interest, they wheeled out a sushi cart right onto Liberty Avenue, much to the shock and wonder of passersby in order to get people asking questions and try something they'd likely never tried before.

It worked. The BYOB restaurant with a sushi bar and a handful of tables serves up exotic and artistic plates of delicacies including *Kona Kampachi* (yellowtail), *ikura* (Skuna Bay salmon roe), and quail eggs to intrigued yinzers from all walks of life. While you won't find the good ole' California roll on Matt's menu, you will find something familiar if you aren't into being adventurous. Salmon and tuna flown in fresh from Japan are sprinkled throughout appetizers and entrees. Indulge in Chocolate Shiitake Ice Cream to wash everything down.

Bringing together house-made seasonings, rice cooked to perfection in a *hangiri* (a very expensive cedar tub), and quality ingredients are of utmost importance to Matt, as is a continual learning process. He teaches apprentices the skills necessary to continue providing this spectacularly wild cuisine in the most organic and beautiful ways possible.

Remember to use your hands for nigiri (rolls), chopsticks for sashimi (thinly sliced raw fish), go easy on the soy, never ever mix your wasabi into said soy, and enjoy a piece of pickled ginger between different varieties of sushi to cleanse your palate.

KUSSHI OYSTERS WITH JUNIPER SHISHO GRANITA, FRESH LEMON & THAI CHILES

SERVES 25 (1 OYSTER PER SERVING)

For the oysters:

25 Kusshi oysters
3 lemons

For the chile oil:

25 grams Thai chiles
75 grams soy oil (or other neutral oil)
Pinch of salt

For the granita:

145 grams granulated sugar
525 grams water
Pinch of salt
8 whole dried juniper berries
175 grams shiso (Japanese beefsteak leaves)
Xanthan gum

Shredded daikon (Japanese radish), for serving
Pickled ginger, for serving

Special equipment:

Metric kitchen scale
Splash guard
Blender
Fine-mesh strainer

To prepare oysters: Clean the oysters by removing sand and mud with a brush then rinsing them under cold water. Store in single rows in a container lined and topped with dampened newspaper. Do not cover with plastic wrap.

Juice the lemons and strain to remove the seeds and pulp. Set aside.

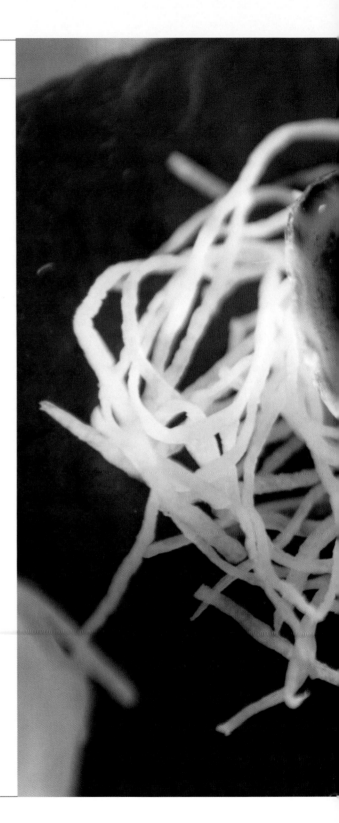

To prepare chile oil: Combine Thai chiles, soy oil, and a pinch of salt in a small pot. Cover with a splash guard. Gently heat the oil until the chiles begin to blister and split. Do not blacken. Cool and blend well. Set aside.

To prepare the granita: Combine sugar and water in a pan and heat until the sugar is dissolved. Take out 241 grams for the recipe and save the rest for later use. Cool thoroughly.

Add salt and juniper berries to a blender and pulse until broken up. Add half of the sugar solution. Slowly add shiso leaves, pulsing until blended. Add remaining sugar solution until mixture becomes thick. Add the rest of the water and slowly add the remainder of the shiso. Once the mixture is uniform, strain it through a fine-mesh strainer.

Weigh the amount of strained liquid. Measure 1 percent of the total weight and add that amount of xanthan gum to the liquid. Mix until thoroughly incorporated. Freeze in a shallow container.

Once solid, scrape the surface with a fork until the mass becomes tiny ice crystals.

To serve: Open the oysters, separating the abductor muscle but leaving it on the half shell. Add a small amount of fresh lemon juice and chile oil to each oyster, and top with granita. Rest on shredded daikon, and serve pickled ginger as a palate cleanser.

Saba with Grilled Cucumber Foam & Pickled Apple Fluid Gel

Serves 20 (3 slices per serving)

For the pickled apple fluid gel:

3 pieces whole star anise
1½ tablespoons whole juniper berries
1½ tablespoons whole coriander seeds
200 milliliters grain (rice) vinegar
¼ cup granulated sugar
½ tablespoon salt
2 tablespoons mirin
600 grams Granny Smith apples, sliced
Powdered gelatin

For the mackerel:

1 Spanish mackerel
Kosher salt
Grain vinegar

For the grilled cucumber foam:

1 medium cucumber
Coarse sea salt
1 clove garlic
Pinch of salt
Pinch of black pepper
Soy lecithin

Shredded daikon

Special equipment:

Metric kitchen scale
Cheesecloth
Fine-mesh strainer
Blender
Knife and tweezers for removing fish bones
Charcoal grill
Aerolatte milk frother
Butane torch

To prepare the pickled apple fluid gel: Place anise, juniper berries, and coriander seeds into a square of cheesecloth, gather up the corners and tie, and set aside. Heat on medium the remaining ingredients except the apple until the sugar and salt dissolve. Strain into a container with the apples. Add the spices tied into cheesecloth and refrigerate the mixture for 24 hours. The next day, puree the mixture and pass it through a fine-mesh strainer. Weigh the mixture and measure 1 percent of the weight; add that amount of gelatin to the mixture. Heat until the gelatin is dissolved. Pour the mixture into a wide, shallow container and cool until the gel is set, about 1 hour. Puree until smooth, adding a small amount of water to get desired consistency, if necessary.

To prepare the mackerel: Remove the head and eviscerate. Remove 2 fillets. Cut off the rib bones with knife and remove the bones down the center of the fillets with tweezers. Salt both sides of the fillets and let rest for 45 minutes, then rinse in cold water until the salt is removed. If you aren't comfortable deboning the mackerel, ask your fishmonger to prepare 2 fillets, bones removed. Place in vinegar just up to the skin for 15 minutes. Rinse well and dry. Heat up a charcoal grill and blister the skin side only above the heat.

To prepare the cucumber foam: Wash cucumber, rubbing it with a little bit of coarse sea salt. Rinse completely and pat dry. Roast over hot charcoal until the skin begins to blacken slightly and blister. Blend with garlic, salt, and pepper and pass through a fine-mesh strainer. Weigh the mixture and measure 1.25 percent of its total weight. Add that amount of soy lecithin and mix thoroughly until incorporated. Use an Aerolatte to create foam for serving.

To serve: Put a smear of the apple fluid gel across the plate. Slice three pieces of mackerel and gently warm them up with a torch, without actually cooking the fish, to enhance flavor.

Arrange on shredded daikon. Spoon a bit of the cucumber foam onto the plate next to the mackerel and serve.

Gaucho Parrilla Argentina

1607 Penn Avenue
Pittsburgh, PA 15222
(412) 709-6622
EATGAUCHO.COM
Owner: Amy Falcon
Chef: Anthony Falcon

Gaucho Parrilla Argentina has somewhat of a cult following. Customers just can't seem to get enough of the traditional Argentinean offerings and come back twice, sometimes three, four, and even five times a week. Chef Anthony Falcon is pleased to know people are enjoying the food and atmosphere enough to come time and time again.

The wood-fired foods range from skirt steak, flank steak, and strip steak to chorizo, shrimp, chicken, and fish. Vegetarians and vegans need not shy away as the menu also is riddled with empanadas, ensaladas, tortillas, and veggies. Gaucho (translated as "cowboy") provides meals that any guy or gal would be eating while out in the South American countryside. Anthony purposely left off a few items from the final menu but hopes to incorporate those interesting and unique dishes once Pittsburghers' palates have adapted enough to the Argentinean spices and cooking methods.

He came up with the idea for Gaucho after working most of his career as a chef at resorts, hotels, and golf clubs. Hailing from South America, he visited the Strip District with his family. They all appreciated the authentic atmosphere the Strip provided but instantly saw a gap in the ethnic cuisine. He knew he needed to go where the action was; thus the first *parrilla* ("grill") in Pittsburgh was born.

Wood stacks fill the majority of the floor space inside, and folks huddled around tall wooden tables fill the rest. With bottles of booze they've brought from home (Gaucho is BYOB), patrons are abuzz with excitement as the scent of campfire wafts through the air.

Outside, a few tables and chairs fill up the courtyard and passersby poke their heads in the open door to see what's happening inside. Anthony takes pride in the restaurant and its surroundings. As he says, "Business owners have a responsibility to contribute to the city and make it as beautiful as they possibly can."

The small staff at Gaucho is all about having fun, building relationships with their customers, and sharing the good food they prepare with anyone who is interested in trying something new. Says Anthony, "We like to give things away. We make these empanadas, and we're like here . . . you have to try this!"

PROVOLETTA

SERVES 1

2 tablespoons extra-virgin olive oil, divided

Pinch of fresh oregano leaves

2 (1-ounce) pieces aged sharp provolone

2 ciabatta bread slices

Pinch of salt

Pinch of fresh ground pepper

A handful of arugula

4 kalamata olives

½ teaspoon lemon juice

Special equipment:

Wood fire

Cast iron chappa (griddle)

Over a wood fire, heat the cast iron chappa to moderately high heat. Drizzle with olive oil, sprinkle on oregano leaves, and place provolone atop the oregano. Cook cheese to dark golden brown on both sides.

Meanwhile, season the ciabatta with olive oil and salt and pepper and toast both sides over low heat coals. Place the browned cheese atop the toast and serve with arugula tossed with olives, lemon juice, and the remaining olive oil.

PIMENTON

MAKES 1 GALLON

For the salmuera ("brine"):

Kosher salt, to taste

4 cups water

For the red pepper puree:

5–8 red peppers

Prepared salmuera

4 cups extra-virgin olive oil

4 cups red wine vinegar

4 cups balsamic vinegar

½ cup chopped garlic

1 tablespoon crushed red pepper flakes

2 cups chopped parsley

Special equipment:

Wood fire

Blender

To prepare the salmuera: Place water in small saucepan and boil. Add salt gradually until dissolved, and continue adding salt and tasting until flavor resembles sea water. Allow to cool.

To prepare the red pepper puree: Slice open and char red peppers over moderately high-heat wood fire. Allow to cool. Process in blender with prepared salmuera on medium until smooth.

To prepare the pimenton: Combine extra-virgin olive oil, red wine vinegar, balsamic vinegar, garlic, red pepper flakes, prepared roasted pepper puree, and parsley together; stir and allow to rest for 1 hour before serving.

Note from the chef: Prepared pimenton can be stored in refrigerator for up to 3 weeks.

ENTRAGNA

SERVES 1

1 piece outside skirt steak
2 tablespoons extra-virgin olive oil
Pinch of kosher salt
Pinch of fresh ground pepper
Chimichurri sauce for serving

Special equipment:

Wood fire
Wood grill

Allow skirt steak to rest at room temperature for 20 minutes prior to cooking. Massage skirt steak with olive oil and season to taste with salt and coarse ground butcher pepper.

Over high heat and in close proximity to flame on a wood grill, grill the meat on both sides for just a few moments until charred and crisp. Entragna is served best medium to medium rare. Slice steak against meat grain and serve immediately with chimichurri sauce.

Habitat

The Fairmont Pittsburgh
510 Market Street
Pittsburgh, PA 15222
(412) 773-8848
habitatrestaurant.com
Executive Chef: Jason Dalling

Jason Dalling's first position within the Fairmont Hotels & Resorts family didn't come by way of an impressive résumé. It came by way of some gutsy, secret-spy-type moves. After stalking open positions and submitting applications to the Fairmont Hotel Macdonald in Edmonton, Alberta, for over a year, he took matters into his own hands. He snuck his way into the building, maneuvered through the back hallways, and found the executive chef's office. Once there, he sat the chef down and rattled off his top-ten reasons why he should be hired. "I told him I was smart enough to get into the building, and I assured him I could outcook every single one of the cooks in his kitchen," says Jason. "I was basically declaring to him that I would do anything it took to be successful." He was hired on the spot.

That was over twenty years ago. Today Jason has advanced his career through multiple Fairmont hotels in both Canada and the United States before landing as the

executive chef at Habitat in late 2012. Born in Vancouver, Jason moved into the mountains of northern British Columbia when he was five. In this wild, rugged terrain, he says he did things that were really, really Canadian, like hunting for wild game, smoking meats, pickling, and preserving. And these everyday tasks of his childhood have influenced him as a chef, from technique to a comfort level working with local farms.

At Habitat, you will find Jason in his comfort zone, turning out internationally inspired plates sourced from local ingredients, such as Alaskan black cod served with roasted cauliflower, golden raisins, pine nuts, lemon, and pickled mushrooms, and house-made pappardelle mixed with duck confit, braised leeks, house-made chorizo, and a coriander *beurre monté*.

In Pittsburgh, he finds the people generous, the city architecturally beautiful, and the landscape paradise. "Everything that chefs love and find hard to get in a city center is here," says Jason. "Local purveyors and great local products are readily available and all around us." And in his kitchen, he finds a young, energetic staff willing to learn from his experiences. Jason affirms that if an eager, fledgling

chef found a way to sneak into his kitchen at Habitat and listed the reasons why he or she should be hired, they probably would be . . . right on the spot.

HOMEMADE DOUGHNUTS & PENNSYLVANIA PEANUT MILK LATTE

SERVES 4

For doughnuts:

2 cups all-purpose flour, plus additional for
    rolling out dough
½ cup granulated sugar, plus additional for
    dusting the fried doughnuts
½ cup milk
2 teaspoons baking powder
¼ teaspoon salt
1 large egg
1 tablespoon unsalted butter, melted
½ teaspoon vanilla extract
Oil for deep-frying

For peanut milk latte:

1 cup unsalted, blanched peanuts
3½ cups whole milk, plus additional for foaming
1¼ cups heavy cream
¼ cup packed dark muscovado sugar or
    dark brown sugar
½ vanilla bean, split lengthwise

Special equipment:

Deep fryer
Blender
Fine-mesh strainer
Milk frother

To prepare the doughnuts: Mix together all-purpose flour, sugar, milk, baking powder, salt, egg, unsalted butter, and vanilla in a mixing bowl until well combined.

Turn the dough out onto a lightly floured surface and knead gently for about 2 minutes or until the dough is smooth. Allow dough to sit at room temperature in the bowl covered with a tea towel for about 30 minutes.

Roll dough out onto a lightly floured surface until it is about ½-inch thick. Cut doughnuts into eight equal-size squares and deep-fry until golden brown. Once removed from the oil, dust with granulated sugar while they are still hot.

To prepare peanut milk latte: Preheat the oven to 350°F.

Roast peanuts in the preheated oven on a rimmed baking sheet, stirring occasionally, until golden, about 15 minutes. Transfer peanuts to a large, heavy, high-sided saucepan. Add milk, cream, and sugar. Scrape in the seeds from

the vanilla bean and add them and the bean to saucepan. Bring to a simmer over medium-low heat and simmer until mixture is reduced by a quarter, about 45 minutes. Remove from heat.

Let steep until cooled to room temperature, about 2 hours. Cover and chill overnight. Remove the vanilla bean from the peanut mixture.

Working in two batches if needed, purée the chilled peanut mixture in a blender on medium-low speed until smooth. Strain through a fine-mesh sieve into a medium pitcher; discard the solids in the sieve. Cover and chill until cold, about 2 hours.

To serve: Reheat the peanut milk to serve and top with foamed milk for a latte-like beverage. Serve with two doughnuts per portion.

BACON & EGGS SALAD

SERVES 4

For the bacon jam:

1 pound bacon
1 medium onion, chopped
3 cloves garlic, chopped
¼ cup apple cider vinegar
½ cup packed dark brown sugar (substitute up to
    ¼ cup with maple syrup to make bacon jam)
1 fresh tomato, chopped
½ cup brewed coffee

For soft-boiled eggs:

4 large eggs

For the toasted croutons:

2 slices whole wheat bread
Olive oil
Salt and pepper to taste

For the asparagus:

8 asparagus spears
Olive oil
Salt and pepper to taste

Frisée

Special equipment:

Grill

To prepare bacon jam: In a large skillet, cook the strips of bacon just until starting to brown and crisp at edges. Remove cooked bacon to paper towel–lined plate to cool and drain off the excess grease. Once the bacon has cooled, cut it into ½ x ½-inch pieces.

Pour out all but 1 tablespoon of bacon fat from the skillet. Turn the heat down to medium-low. Add onions and garlic. Cook until onions are translucent. Add vinegar, brown sugar, tomato, and coffee. Bring mixture to a boil. Add cooked, chopped bacon and return to a low simmer. Continue to cook the mixture slowly, stirring occasionally until it has a thickened and jam-like consistency. Remove from the heat and reserve at room temperature.

To prepare soft-boiled eggs: Bring a pot of water to a boil, carefully add 4 eggs with a slotted spoon, and time for 6 minutes. Immediately plunge the eggs into ice water until chilled. Carefully remove shell from eggs and reserve until plating.

To prepare the toasted croutons: Preheat oven to 350°F.

Remove the crust from 2 slices of whole wheat bread and discard. Cut the remaining bread into ¼ x ¼-inch cubes. Gently toss with a small amount of olive oil, salt, and pepper. Place croutons on a baking sheet and place in oven for approximately 5 to 6 minutes or until lightly toasted. Remove from the oven and reserve.

To prepare the asparagus: Season asparagus with olive oil, salt, and pepper and grill lightly until cooked through. Once cooled, cut asparagus spears into 4-inch lengths and reserve.

To serve: Form quenelles with 2 tablespoons of bacon jam. Place 2 quenelles of bacon jam on opposite sides of each plate. Carefully cut each soft-boiled egg in half, and place half next to each portion of bacon jam. Place 1 asparagus spear leaning against each portion of bacon jam. Arrange a small amount of frisée lettuce and a few croutons as a garnish to each arrangement and serve.

KALEIDOSCOPE CAFE

108 43RD STREET
PITTSBURGH, PA 15201
(412) 683-4004
KALEIDOSCOPEPGH.COM
CHEF/OWNER: DAN ROBINSON

Sometimes the simplest things change you. For Dan Robinson, it was five simple words.

Dan started working in the restaurant business at the age of fifteen. And after attempts to discover his passions at California University of Pennsylvania and the Art Institute of Pittsburgh, he finally found clarity. It came when Morgan Freeman said, "You do what you are" in the movie *Along Came a Spider*. "It was the moment I decided being a chef was what I wanted to do," says Dan. Soon after that epiphany, Dan became part owner of his first restaurant.

He eventually sold his part of the restaurant to travel the world. Twenty-six countries and a run-in with a silverback gorilla later, Dan was searching for his next move. That's when fate stepped in. While scouting restaurant locations, an unexpected detour lead him to Lawrenceville.

Enter, Kaleidoscope Cafe.

The thirty-six-seat, eclectic American restaurant is a work of art inside and out.

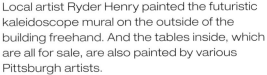

Local artist Ryder Henry painted the futuristic kaleidoscope mural on the outside of the building freehand. And the tables inside, which are all for sale, are also painted by various Pittsburgh artists.

Dan doesn't have formal culinary training so he says his technique "toolbox" is basic. But don't let that fool you. The menu is anything but basic. Duck cannoli: roasted duck stuffed inside a homemade cannoli and served with a white chocolate cardamom beurre blanc and pistachio dust is his favorite thing to prepare. "I love duck. If I won the lottery I'd have a duck farm with a bed-and-breakfast on it. I'd make all kinds of duck. Free-range ducks that I would love, kill, and eat," says Dan with a laugh.

He's also perfected the art of deep-frying gnocchi. Yes, deep-frying gnocchi. Either tossed with fresh herbs, Romano cheese, and house-made marinara or with chorizo and *kafta* (an Indian-spiced tomato-cashew sauce), these delicate pillows will melt in your mouth.

Deep-Fried Gnocchi with Marinara

SERVES 6–8

For the marinara:

4–6 cloves garlic
¼ cup olive oil
1 (10-ounce) can Italian tomatoes
2 bunches fresh basil, leaves removed
     and stems discarded
Salt and pepper to taste

For the gnocchi:

3–4 medium-size potatoes
1 egg
5 heaping tablespoons grated Romano cheese
Salt and pepper to taste
1½ cups all-purpose flour, plus additional for
     rolling out gnocchi
Oil for deep-frying

Special equipment:

Ricer
Stand mixer with paddle attachment
Deep fryer

To prepare the marinara: Slice the garlic as thin
as possible. Put olive oil in a large saucepan over
low heat and add the sliced garlic to the oil. Let
the garlic permeate the oil, but do not let it brown.
Add tomatoes and let simmer for about 2 hours,
stirring often and crushing tomatoes as you do
so. Chop basil and add to the sauce and season
with salt and pepper to taste.

To prepare the gnocchi: Peel and cut potatoes
into uniform cubes. Boil potatoes until a knife will
pass through them easily. Drain the potatoes
and let dry on a sheet tray. Once potatoes are
completely dry, push them through a ricer.

Combine the potatoes, egg, cheese (reserving
1 tablespoon to toss with your finished gnocchi),
and salt and pepper in a stand mixer with a
paddle attachment. Mix on slow. Slowly add
small amounts of flour until the dough starts to
hold together and pull away from the sides of the
mixer. Do not overmix.

Dust a large cutting board with flour, roll out
"snakes" of dough about the thickness of your
thumb, and cut pieces about ¾-inch in length.
Continue to lightly dust your cutting board with
flour. Drop the gnocchi into a deep fryer set at
350°F until golden brown. Drain on paper towel
for about 1 minute then toss with the remaining
Romano cheese.

Duck Cannoli with White Chocolate Cardamom Beurre Blanc, Candied Orange Peel & Pistachio Dust

SERVES 4

1 whole duck

For white chocolate cardamom beurre blanc sauce:

1–2 shallots
3 cups white wine
1 cup cardamom pods (see note)
¼ cup white chocolate chips
4 tablespoons (½ stick) unsalted butter

For candied orange peel:

1 orange
3 cups sugar
1 cup water

4–6 cannoli shells
½ cup shelled pistachios, crushed

To prepare the duck: Preheat the oven to 475°F.

Cut the duck down the middle of the breastbone using kitchen shears. Remove the neck and any organs inside. Open the duck so it lies flat in a roasting pan, cavity side down. Place the duck in the oven, uncovered, for 20 minutes. Decrease temperature to 300°F, cover duck, and put back in oven for 2½ hours.

To check for doneness, gently wiggle the leg of the duck. If it seems as though you can easily remove the bone from the meat, then the duck is done. If it feels tight and connected, continue cooking. When finished, drain the fat and let the duck rest for 15 to 20 minutes. Remove the skin and pull the meat from the bones.

To prepare white chocolate cardamom beurre blanc sauce: Peel and mince the shallots and place in a saucepan. Add wine and cardamom pods and reduce almost to an al sec (a syrupy consistency). Remove from heat and immediately add white chocolate to the saucepan. Rapidly stir in butter while pan is still warm to give sauce a glossy appearance.

To prepare candied orange peel: Peel the orange, being careful to not include too much of the white pith. Cut the peel into strips. Boil the strips and stop the cooking by submerging them in cold water. Combine sugar and water into small saucepan and heat until sugar is dissolved. Add peels to the saucepan and let simmer for about 2 to 3 minutes. Remove the peels and let dry.

To serve: Stuff each side of the cannoli shells with pulled duck meat. Drizzle sauce around plate and top with candied orange peel and crushed pistachios.

Note from the chef: Add cardamom pods to the white wine at least 1 day before preparing the rest of the dish.

LET'S GET VISUAL

Feeding the need for culture is an easy task in Pittsburgh. Theaters are aplenty in the Cultural District of Downtown, complete with operas, and ballets, and musicals—oh my! The visual arts get their due at galleries around the city, and three big institutions reign supreme: The Mattress Factory, The Andy Warhol Museum, and Carnegie Museum of Art.

The Mattress Factory (mattressfactory.org) is an installation art museum in the Northside neighborhood. This can't-miss spot's motto is "Art you can get into." Room after room of site-specific work proves this to be true. Stand among dots and mirrors inside Yayoi Kusama's *Infinity Dots Mirrored Room* or sit in darkness to experience James Turrell's *Pleiades*.

Check out Pittsburgh's famous native son, Andy Warhol, at The Warhol on the North Shore (warhol.org). The museum showcases Warhol's work in spades and features exhibitions that play off Warholian themes and inspiration. Marilyn and Elvis are permanent residents on the walls.

Carnegie Museum of Art (cmoa.org) has a little something for everyone, from ancient arts to contemporary color fields. Plus admission here allows visitors access to both the art museum and The Carnegie Museum of Natural History. Degas and dinos suddenly go hand in hand.

For information about theaters and offerings in the Cultural District, visit trustarts.org.

LA GOURMANDINE BAKERY & PASTRY SHOP

4605 BUTLER STREET
PITTSBURGH, PA 15201
(412) 682-2210
LAGOURMANDINEBAKERY.COM
CHEF/OWNER: FABIEN MOREAU
OWNER: LISANNE MOREAU

"Some say about northern France, that you'll cry twice while there. Once when you arrive and once when you leave." A sweet sentiment spoken by a sweet man from the sweetest bakery west of Paris.

Fabien Moreau and his wife, Lisanne, left fair France behind some years ago and landed in Pittsburgh. Wanting to bring French culture to Lawrenceville's up-and-coming neighborhood, which reminded them so much of the energetic and diverse European streets, they hatched a plan to pop up a classic Parisian bakery right on Butler Street.

Best known for their lemon tarts, almond croissants, and quiches, La Gourmandine also sells various savories, freshly baked brioche, and house-made soups. Pittsburghers, more familiar with Polish, Italian, and Irish grub, have welcomed these traditional French delicacies.

While they now call the 'Burgh home, Fabien and his family travel to France often, where they rejuvenate their palates and absorb fresh ideas for presenting beautiful confectionaries. Because baking is so precise, Fabien follows recipes to a tee as not to disrupt the flow or outcome of his creations. The flexibility comes with decorating and displaying the petit fours, tartlettes, and Danishes. His day begins early, and when the tricky Danish delights go off without a hitch, he knows the day will be a success.

The sight of a packed house and possible lines out the door may deter passersby from wanting to go anywhere near La Gourmandine, but one step inside, one deep breath to fill your lungs with the scents of baking breads, and the sight of beautifully arranged pastries dusted with the perfect amount of confectioners' sugar, and you'll be glad you didn't stay away.

Verrine Fraise & Mascarpone

MAKES 12 SHOT GLASSES

For the strawberry bavarois:

7 grams gelatin sheet
Cold water
219 grams strawberry coulis (strawberry sauce)
44 grams egg yolks
66 grams sugar
220 grams heavy cream

For the mascarpone mousse:

250 grams mascarpone
50 grams confectioners' sugar
90 grams egg whites

Fresh strawberries for garnish

Special equipment:

Metric kitchen scale
Candy thermometer
Pastry bag

To prepare the strawberry bavarois: Put the gelatin sheets in cold water. In a saucepan, mix together coulis, egg yolks, and sugar. Very slowly, cook ingredients until 177°F. Drain the gelatin and add it to the coulis mixture. Cool down to 77°F. In a bowl, whip heavy cream until soft peaks form and fold it into coulis. Refrigerate until used.

To prepare the mascarpone mousse: In a bowl, mix the mascarpone and confectioners' sugar together with a whisk. In a separate bowl, beat egg whites with a hand mixer until soft peaks form. Incorporate the whipped egg whites into the mascarpone-sugar mixture.

To serve: In a shot glass, use a pastry bag to pipe some of the mascarpone mousse on the bottom. Add fresh berry slices and cover everything with the strawberry bavarois. Let firm for an hour in the refrigerator.

Garnish with more fresh strawberries.

MADELEINES

MAKES 16 COOKIES

100 grams unsalted butter, plus additional
    for greasing the pan
175 grams white sugar
125 grams eggs
200 grams all-purpose flour
8 grams baking powder
100 grams milk

Special equipment:

Metric kitchen scale
Madeleine pan
Stand mixer with paddle attachment (optional)
Pastry bag
Convection oven

Preheat oven to 350°F. Grease molds or madeleine pan.

Melt the butter in a saucepan and let it cool.

Mix sugar and eggs with a paddle, if using a stand mixer, or with a wooden spoon if mixing by hand. Add the flour and baking powder and mix until a paste forms. Slowly add the milk. Finish by adding the cooled butter.

Using a pastry bag, pipe 60 grams of the batter into each mold. Cook in a convection oven for 6 minutes at 350°F, rotate, and cook 5 more minutes at 325°F.

LEGENDS OF THE NORTH SHORE

500 EAST NORTH AVENUE
PITTSBURGH, PA 15212
(412) 321-8000
LEGENDSATTHENORTHSHORE.COM
CHEF/OWNER: DAN BARTOW

Growing up on Long Island has given Chef Dan Bartow a special appreciation for Neapolitan-style fare. He'd need only turn around in New York City and bump into at least a dozen kosher delis, pizzerias, and traditional pasta joints "everywheres." The food he'd become accustomed to wasn't complicated in nature. His favorite dishes were prepared passionately with quality ingredients and served up with classic Italian flare.

When Dan accompanied his wife back to her hometown of Pittsburgh, he knew he may need to kiss his love of fresh fish, secret sauces, and pasta aplenty goodbye. Or would he? He took his experience with Neapolitan food and opened Legends of the North Shore in 2002. The carefully restored Northside building features a bar with seats for just a few and a modest dining room not nearly large enough to hold the burgeoning crowds.

Dan feeds people what he likes to eat, so technically his menu is entirely chef approved. A gardener by nature, he has an appreciation for the work that goes into

preparing a great meal. You can find him scouring the historic Strip District for the freshest produce. He then takes it back to the kitchen where he pairs it with his freshly baked breads, homemade sauces, and the seafood he has shipped in from the best corners of the world.

His core menu offers something for everyone, including his award-winning spaghetti and meatballs, the fan-favorite penne vodka with prosciutto, and what just may be his claim to fame, Mama's Gravy. Not really gravy at all, the thick red sauce is spiced to perfection and readily available for pouring, dunking, and scooping. Mama's Gravy is so admired among patrons that it just might make its way into bottles available for purchase.

Dan's specials are what really sell Legends. "A benefit of a chef-owned restaurant is that you have the ability to prepare food differently," Dan says. "You aren't stuck with a static menu; you can adapt with the season and be a little adventurous with your cooking."

The energetic vibe of the urban Northside drew Dan in and reminded him of his roots in Long Island, so there's a little bit of home here with him, a sentiment you can fully appreciate as you taste his authentic cooking.

ORECCHIETTE VODKA & CHICKEN

SERVES 4

3 cloves garlic

2 tablespoons olive oil

¼ cup white wine

1 cup whipping cream

4 cups tomato sauce

½ cup grated Parmigiano Reggiano or Romano cheese

Salt and freshly ground pepper to taste

1 pound orecchiette pasta

¾ cup vodka

6 whole thin slices prosciutto

2 cups diced cooked boneless chicken breast

Sauté garlic in olive oil for 1 minute. Add wine and simmer for another minute. Add the cream, tomato sauce, cheese, and salt and pepper. Let simmer on low.

Prepare the orecchiette pasta by bringing a large pot of lightly salted water to a boil. Cook the pasta for 10 to 12 minutes. Drain.

Add vodka to the sauce and stir. Mix in prosciutto and chicken. Pour over pasta and enjoy!

BEANS & GREENS

SERVES 2

¼ cup olive oil

1 cup spring mix salad greens

1 cup baby escarole greens

1 cup baby spinach leaves

Salt and freshly ground pepper to taste

Pinch of crushed red pepper

3 cloves garlic, minced

2 cups cannellini beans, drained and rinsed

½ cup chicken stock

½ cup grated Romano or Parmigiano Reggiano cheese

Heat olive oil in large skillet over medium heat. Add the spring mix, baby escarole, and baby spinach. The greens will crackle and start to wilt. Using tongs, toss for 3 to 4 minutes. Season with salt, pepper, and red pepper to taste.

Add garlic and toss. Add cannellini beans and toss again. Lastly add chicken stock and toss.

Sprinkle in cheese and blend. Serve immediately.

Gnocchi with Broccoli Rabe

SERVES 4

For the gnocchi:

6 potatoes
3 cups flour
2 egg yolks
¾ cup Parmigiano Reggiano or Romano cheese
Salt and freshly ground pepper to taste

For the broccoli rabe:

3 pounds broccoli rabe
½ cup olive oil
3 cloves garlic, minced
1 cup water
Salt and pepper to taste

1 cup Parmigiano Reggiano or Romano cheese

Special equipment:

Ricer

To prepare the gnocchi: Bring a pot of salted water to a boil. Cut the potatoes in half and add to the boiling water. Boil 12 to 15 minutes, then drain. Peel and puree potatoes through a ricer. Form dough by mixing the potato puree with the flour, egg yolks, cheese, salt, and pepper.

Roll the dough into long ropelike strips. Cut the strips into bite-size pieces and set aside.

Cook gnocchi in boiling salted water until they float, then drain.

To prepare broccoli rabe: Chop broccoli rabe into bite-size pieces.

Heat olive oil in a pan over medium heat. Add broccoli rabe pieces to the olive oil. Add garlic, water, and salt and pepper. Cook for 20 minutes, adding more water if needed.

Mix gnocchi with broccoli rabe and toss gently until gnocchi are coated. Top with freshly grated cheese. Serve immediately.

LEGUME

214 NORTH CRAIG STREET
PITTSBURGH, PA 15213
(412) 621-2700
LEGUMEBISTRO.COM
CHEF/OWNER: TREVETT HOOPER
OWNER: SARAH HOOPER

If Trevett Hooper was a superhero, he would don a chef's coat and cape and call himself "Nutrition Man." His superpower: creating beautiful, nourishing plates of food.

And in his real-world kitchen at Legume, that is just what he does, minus the cape.

Here you are going to find an ever-changing menu of honest plates of food, such as lentils with garlicky goat sausage and mushroom barley risotto with roasted beef sirloin. "What I do really well is make viscerally good food," says Trevett. "Food that tastes good, looks beautiful, and will make you feel really good two hours later."

In the early 1990s, Trevett found himself glued to his television watching the show *Great Chefs, Great Cities* and thought to himself, "Wow, that looks like so much fun!" In college, he got to experience that fun with his first job in a kitchen. He says he loved being in that kitchen, escaping from student life and watching the chef make her own veal stock and breads. By the time college graduation came around, Trevett knew he was destined to be a chef. He talked his way into kitchens in Boston and San Diego before moving back to Pittsburgh with his wife, Sarah, in 2007 to open Legume in Regent Square. "I just wanted to do really straightforward food that was really flavorful and healthy," says Trevett. As time went on, he got more ambitious and grew Legume into the current eighty-five-seat restaurant and bar Butterjoint (see page 113), in North Oakland. He says the move has been a natural progression to a neighborhood that he absolutely loves.

When not in the kitchen as "Nutrition Man," Trevett is at home with his wife and kids, who think he is "Super Dad."

STINGING NETTLES SOUP

MAKES 2 QUARTS

This is made at Legume in the spring and fall, the two times of the year when nettles are available in western Pennsylvania.

8 ounces russet potatoes, cubed

4 ounces leeks, chopped

¼ cup olive oil

5 cups chicken or vegetable stock

8 ounces stinging nettles

Salt and pepper to taste

2 tablespoons chopped fresh chives

½ cup crème fraîche or sour cream

Special equipment:

Blender

In a bowl, soak the cubed potatoes in water for 10 minutes to remove some of the starch.

Cook leeks in olive oil in a stockpot until soft. Add potatoes and stock and bring to a boil. Simmer for 15 minutes. Add nettles and cook for 5 more minutes. Puree in a blender and season with salt and pepper. Adjust consistency with extra stock or water if the soup is too thick.

Make chive crème fraîche by mixing together chives and crème fraîche (or sour cream) in a separate bowl. Pour soup into serving bowls and swirl crème fraîche (or sour cream) into the soup.

BUTTERJOINT

214 NORTH CRAIG STREET
PITTSBURGH, PA 15213
(412) 621-2700
THEBUTTERJOINT.COM

At Legume, you might think of a vegetable-heavy menu, but breaking down whole animals is a big thing in the kitchen. And Trevett Hooper says when you break down whole animals, you end up with a lot of leftover meat. Enter Butterjoint, the cozy watering hole adjacent to Legume's dining room serving up casual comfort food. Think daily, fresh-ground burgers with fries, house-made sausage, pierogies stuffed with potatoes and farmer's cheese, and fried sauerkraut balls served with honey-mustard mayo.

Butterjoint allows Legume's customers who may only visit the restaurant once or twice a year to experience what Trevett and his kitchen are doing on a more frequent and affordable basis. "Over the years, we have gotten more expensive as we have gotten more ambitious," says Trevett. "With Butterjoint, we wanted to make sure our customers who absolutely love what we are doing and believe in us could come more often."

And the name? Not named after a dairy product, this bar is named after a masonry term, *butter joint,* in which bricks are laid closely together with thin mortar. This type of masonry can be found all over the North Oakland neighborhood and reflects the style of cooking at Butterjoint: simple in theory but requiring an intense level of detail for proper execution.

Rum & Apple Shrub

MAKES 1 COCKTAIL

For the apple shrub (makes 1 quart):

2 pounds apples, mixed varieties, roughly chopped

4 cups granulated sugar

2 pints apple cider vinegar

6 cinnamon sticks, divided

1 teaspoon grains of paradise, cracked

For the cocktail:

2 ounces rum (Mount Gay Eclipse preferred)

2 ounces apple shrub (see above)

Ice

Dusting of ground cinnamon, for garnish

Special equipment:

Cocktail shaker

To prepare the apple shrub: Combine the apples and sugar in a large container. Let stand in a cool, dark place for 1 to 2 days until liquid is extracted from apples and most of the sugar dissolves; not all may dissolve. Strain the apples and reserve the liquid. Combine the solids with vinegar, 3 cinnamon sticks, and grains of paradise in a stockpot. Bring to a simmer and maintain the simmer for 20 minutes. Strain again and discard the solids. Add the reserved sugar syrup from the apples and the 3 remaining cinnamon sticks to the vinegar mixture. Let stand again, refrigerated, for at least 5 days.

To prepare the cocktail: Add rum and shrub to a cocktail shaker. Fill halfway with ice and shake for 5 to 6 seconds. Strain over fresh ice in a double old-fashioned glass. Dust with ground cinnamon.

Note from the chef: The apple shrub recipe makes 1 quart, which will produce a lot of cocktails. Trevett says you might as well make a lot of leftovers if you are going to do all of the work. Leftovers will keep for up to one month in the refrigerator.

Meat & Potatoes

649 Penn Avenue
Pittsburgh, PA 15222
(412) 325-7007
MEATANDPOTATOESPGH.COM
Chef/Owner: Richard DeShantz
Owner: Tolga Sevdik

"I never thought I would actually start cooking," says Richard DeShantz. "I always thought I was going to be an artist." And an artist he is, both in the back and in the front of the house at his Downtown gastropub, Meat & Potatoes. In the back, he works the line, creating welcoming plates of comfort food such as bone marrow, burgers on house-made buns, and of course steak. And, in the front of the house, he designed everything, from painting and construction (with the help of his brother), to picking out the bentwood bar stools and ordering zinc from California to build the tables. "Hopefully someday all I do is create and design and not have to work the line," says Richard.

Working the line is what he has done since the age of fifteen. Richard started out in his uncle's Americanized Italian restaurant working forty to fifty hours a week during high school. After culinary school and an internship at Hyeholde Restaurant in Moon Township, Richard hopped around, working in kitchens in Puerto Rico and Colorado, and he spent a summer staging across the United States, from Texas to Chicago . . . living in a tent. "You know when you sleep in a tent in Colorado it's called camping," says Richard. "Here it's called homeless." It was a job offer from the Hyeholde that brought him back to Pittsburgh.

After three years back at the Hyeholde, Richard set out on his own pursuits. He helped open a wholesale bread company, Mediterra Bakehouse, in which he did everything from build the ovens to bake the bread, often working from 1 a.m. until 5 p.m. the next afternoon. He did this for about four years and then decided it was time to do his own thing. His solo mark in the Pittsburgh culinary scene was Café Richard in the Strip District, then came his first Downtown restaurant, Nine on Nine. Now Richard is focused on his second Downtown restaurant, Meat & Potatoes, which has been jam-packed with patrons since the doors opened in spring 2011.

As a Downtown resident (not living in a tent) and business owner, Richard is a huge supporter of revitalizing Downtown. "Tolga and I walk around, and I tell him all the time, 'You know what I would put in this alley? What about a kiosk serving soft-serve ice cream and burgers over there?'"

Pot Roast with Mashed Potatoes

SERVES 8–10

For the pot roast:

5 pounds chuck blade roast

Olive oil

Salt and pepper to taste

4 diced carrots, roughly chopped on the bias
    in 1-inch pieces

2 onions, diced into large pieces

4 diced celery stalks, roughly chopped
    on the bias in 1-inch pieces

4 cups diced tomatoes

1 bulb garlic

5 sprigs rosemary

5 sprigs thyme

2 cups red wine

Chicken stock, to cover roast

For mashed potatoes:

3 pounds Yukon Gold potatoes, peeled

Salt to taste

½ pound (2 sticks) unsalted butter

1–1½ cups crème fraîche

Salt and pepper to taste

Special equipment:

Ricer

To prepare the pot roast: Preheat the oven to 550°F.

Rub the roast with olive oil and season with salt and pepper. Place the roast on a roasting rack in a roasting pan and place in the oven for 20 minutes or until the roast has a deep brown color. Take the roast out of oven and let it rest.

Turn the oven down to 350°F. In a pot large enough to fit the roast, put a layer of carrots, onions, and celery on the bottom. Set the roast on top and put the remaining vegetables in the pot. Add the garlic bulb, rosemary, thyme, and red wine. Add chicken stock to completely cover the roast. Cover and place in the oven for about 3 hours or until the roast is tender. Remove from oven. Pull roast out of liquid. Take out rosemary and thyme, and discard. Put the pot on medium-high heat on the stove and reduce the liquid by half. Season with salt and pepper to taste. Put roast back into liquid and keep warm until ready to serve.

To prepare the mashed potatoes: Boil the potatoes in a pot of salted water until they are fork tender, about 30 minutes. Strain the potatoes and put them through a ricer. While potatoes are still hot, whip in the butter and then add crème fraîche. Season with salt and pepper to taste.

PÂTÉ DE CHAMPAGNE

SERVES 4–6

2 whole eggs
2 tablespoons all-purpose flour
½ cup heavy cream
2 tablespoons brandy
4 ounces chicken liver
2 pounds pork butt, ground
¼ cup minced onion
8 tablespoons minced parsley
1½ tablespoons minced garlic
4 teaspoons salt
1 teaspoon pepper
½ teaspoon pâté spice

Special equipment:

Food processor
1½-quart long rectangular terrine mold
Meat thermometer

Preheat oven to 300°F.

In a bowl, whisk together eggs, flour, heavy cream, and brandy. Grind chicken liver into paste in food processor. Add ground chicken liver, ground pork butt, minced onion, minced parsley, minced garlic, salt, pepper, and pâté spice into the bowl and mix together to combine.

Line a terrine mold with plastic wrap, leaving a large overhang on all sides. Fill prepared mold with the mixture and tap the mold on the table to remove excess air. Wrap the remaining plastic wrap over the mold and poke holes into the plastic to allow any excess air to escape.

Bake in a water bath for about 1 hour or until the internal temperature reaches 160°F.

Note from the chef: Pâté spice is sold in stores, but also can be made at home by combining: 1 teaspoon ground clove, 1 teaspoon ground nutmeg, 1 teaspoon ground ginger, 1 teaspoon ground coriander, 2 teaspoons ground cinnamon, and 1 tablespoon white pepper.

BUTCHER SHOP 101

MARTY'S MARKET IN THE STRIP DISTRICT
2301 SMALLMAN STREET
PITTSBURGH, PA 15222
(412) 586-7177
MARTYSMARKET.COM

Butcher shops can be intimidating. So many varieties and cuts of meat, most of which you wouldn't ever dream of figuring out how to use. Steve Beachy, the butcher at Marty's Market in the Strip District, has a few tips that will help you feel like an expert anytime you walk into a butcher shop.

Why should I buy meat from a butcher shop?

You're in charge. And you can't beat the quality of the product. "Getting your meat from a butcher allows you to buy exactly what you want, how you want it, and the quantity that you want," says Steve. Plus you get to ask questions about how it was raised.

It's all about relationships.

Find a good butcher shop and develop a relationship with the butcher. Like any great friendship, if you scratch their back, they'll scratch yours . . . and their scratches come in the form of special treatment like knowing your preferences, saving you special cuts of meat, and more.

Don't be afraid to ask questions.

Your butcher is a great resource for cooking tips. They work with the various cuts of meat all day, every day so they'll know what cut is best for your particular recipe.

What cut of meat should you buy?

Steve says a good general rule of thumb is "the more an animal uses a muscle, the tougher it is going to be. These cuts require long and slow cooking. The muscles in the rib and loin section are less used, so they make excellent steaks to be cooked short and fast." So for example chuck roast is good for roasting, stewing, or braising (long and slow). Flank steak is good for grilling or pan searing (short and fast). Brisket is good for smoking, braising, corned beef, or pastrami (long and slow).

What does aging, grading, and marbling mean?

Aging is the time between when the animal is slaughtered and when it is sold to be cooked. Meat is aged to let the enzymes in the meat break down the protein, resulting in a more tender cut. Beef can be aged from a few days to a month or more. *Grading* is determined by the amount of marbling found in the rib of a steer. The best grading is USDA Prime, followed by USDA Choice. *Marbling* is the amount of fat found dispersed within a single muscle. Steak that is well marbled barely has to be touched to make it turn out perfectly.

The butchers at Marty's Market subscribe to the "nose to tail" philosophy, meaning they use every part of the animal being butchered. Things like beef cheeks, marrow bones, duck *rillettes,* game birds, leg of lamb, and house-made sausages are readily available to accommodate any recipe you might be cooking up. So walk up to the butcher counter with confidence and talk to Steve and his team.

Monterey Pub

1227 Monterey Street
Pittsburgh, PA 15212
(412) 322-6535
MONTEREYPUB.COM
Owners: Nancy McMahon and Mark Wade

Nancy McMahon and Mark Wade live on Monterey Street. The nurse and attorney love the neighborhood and their neighbors. When they purchased the restaurant space at 1227 Monterey, they wanted to create a place where friends could gather and feel welcome. Over a decade later, this Irish pub is a second living room to a host of locals.

"It is really like the neighborhood owns this place," Nancy beams. Even the lampshades were a customer purchase. "I came in one day and all of our lights above the tables had new lampshades. One of our regulars bought them and redecorated the light fixtures."

This family pride extends to the staff and food. Mara McDonough, the manager and server, has been on staff almost as long as Monterey Pub's doors have been open. The menu features desserts made by her mother, which change daily depending on what mom wants to make. The Pub favorite is the Hoochie Bar, a chocolate chip cookie with

cream cheese filling and another cookie on top for good measure. The menu also hosts a variety of staff-created items like Mara's grilled cheese (American, cheddar, Monterey Jack, cream cheese, and bacon) and the kitchen's Will Smith's Stoner Pie (chicken on potatoes with cheese). It changes once per year, but the Irish staples like fish-and-chips and the Guinness-infused shepherd's pie remain. All of the bread is sourced from their neighborhood-based bakery, BreadWorks Bakery, and the meat comes from Tom Friday's Market, a stone's throw away.

Nancy and Mark fittingly had a friend create the sign that hangs inside of the front window. Underneath MONTEREY PUB reads, FÁILTE, an Irish "welcome," which is really more a statement of fact than a greeting here. As Mara notes, "People come here once, and they experience the atmosphere. They always come back."

PUB-STYLE SHEPHERD'S PIE

SERVES 4

For the shredded beef:

2 pounds beef knuckle, peeled

1 tablespoon Montreal Steak Seasoning

1 cup Frank's Red Hot sauce

1 pint Guinness

¼ cup A-1 Sauce

1 cup barbecue sauce (Sweet Baby Ray's preferred)

1 cup honey

For the garlic smashed potatoes:

2 pounds red-skin potatoes

4 ounces (1 stick) butter

1 cup heavy cream

1 tablespoon granulated garlic

1 tablespoon chives

Salt and pepper to taste

1 small onion, diced

1 small carrot, diced

Vegetable oil for sauté

8 ounces vegetable mixture (green beans, lima beans, peas, and corn)

8 ounces cheddar cheese, shredded

To prepare the shredded beef: Preheat oven to 350°F.

Coat the beef knuckle with the steak seasoning. Sear off peeled knuckle then place in roasting pan. Add Frank's Red Hot, Guinness, A-1, barbecue sauce, and honey. Cover and cook in the oven for 5 hours.

To prepare the garlic smashed potatoes: Boil potatoes for 30 minutes or until tender. Drain potatoes then place them back in the pot used for boiling. Add butter, heavy cream, granulated garlic, chives, salt, and pepper. Mash to the desired texture.

To prepare the vegetables: Add the onion and carrot to a separate pan and sauté in oil for 5 minutes. Add remaining vegetables and sauté for 5 minutes.

Once the beef has been in the oven for 5 hours, remove it from the roasting pan and shred it into short strands with a fork. Add beef and 2 cups of the au jus from the roast into the pot with the vegetables. Cook on low heat for 5 minutes.

To assemble the pie: Portion the beef and vegetables into four large serving bowls. Add a layer of garlic smashed potatoes covering the meat and vegetables.

Top with a layer of shredded cheddar cheese. Place in oven or under broiler until cheese melts and serve immediately.

Notion

128 South Highland Avenue
Pittsburgh, PA 15206
(412) 361-1188
notionrestaurant.com
Chef/Owner: Dave Racicot

Being a chef is hard work. Let's face it, you pour your heart and soul into each dish you create in the hopes that whoever is lifting the fork to their lips says, "Yum." Nowadays diners have come to expect more out of restaurants. Restaurateurs are striving to obtain the freshest, highest quality ingredients from local sources. Chefs are constantly pushing themselves to think of innovative meals that feature seasonal fruits and vegetables. They are plating works of art, not just food meant to nourish the body.

Few know better than Dave Racicot just how challenging it can be to meet the ever-changing expectations of patrons. Dave is a self-taught chef who claims he doesn't know how to do anything else. Good thing for Pittsburgh that he is exercising his one talent here. He walks the fine line between confident and carefree impeccably well. He exudes an air of honesty while remaining humble and optimistic.

Notion, in Pittsburgh's East End neighborhood, isn't Dave's first restaurant. Dave is no stranger to success or setbacks. Life happened. And a series of events led to him to the "notion" of bringing a new style of cuisine to East Liberty.

The prix-fixe menu is comprised of some of Dave's favorite go-to fare, like the tartare, that goes over well with most folks. But he is confident in his ability to impose something new, exciting, and tantalizingly tasty upon people. One such nouveau dish is scallops that imitate gnocchi paired with Parmesan, English peas, and mint.

The notion that food is an art form that is to be adapted at every possible chance, and the simple hope that even the finickiest of eaters will say "yum" when they fork a bite of food into their expectant faces is what keeps Dave chugging along at top speed. The notion that he's providing a dining experience for people, one where dining out is a night out on the town, makes up for all that hard work.

ESPELETTE PEPPER CREAM

MAKES 560 GRAMS

30 grams shallot, chopped
7 grams garlic, chopped
2 tablespoons olive oil
100 grams vermouth
400 grams half-and-half
3 grams Espelette (chile) pepper
5 grams salt
12 grams sugar
0.4 gram xanthan gum
15 drops fennel extract

Special equipment:

Metric kitchen scale
Blender

Sweat shallot and garlic in 2 tablespoons oil until tender. Add vermouth and reduce by half. Add half-and-half, Espelette pepper, salt, and sugar. Bring to boil. Remove from heat, allow to cool, and add to a blender. With the blender on, slowly add xanthan gum and fennel extract until all ingredients are blended.

Serve with the meat of your choice.

GREEN GODDESS DRESSING

MAKES 548 GRAMS

55 grams egg yolk
100 grams water
25 grams fresh-squeezed lemon juice
1 vanilla bean
9 grams parsley leaves, chopped
9 grams tarragon leaves, chopped
1.5 grams xanthan gum
350 grams salad oil

Special equipment:

Metric kitchen scale
Blender

Place egg yolk, water, lemon juice, vanilla bean (seeds only), parsley, and tarragon in a blender. With the blender running, slowly add xanthan gum. Once incorporated, slowly add salad oil and blend until smooth.

Green goddess dressing pairs perfectly with your favorite seafood or salad.

Osteria 2350

2350 Railroad Street
Pittsburgh, PA 15222
(412) 281-6595
osteria2350pittsburgh.com
Executive·Chef: Greg Alauzen

At fifteen years old, Chef Greg Alauzen started working in his first kitchen at a small mom-and-pop Italian restaurant in the South Hills of Pittsburgh. His mission was simple: to make some cash while in high school. While there, he became allured by the fancy cars the chefs were driving. He thought to himself, "Maybe the chef thing is a good idea."

And after thirty-one years in the chef game, Greg still thinks the whole chef thing is a good idea. At Osteria 2350 in the Strip District, Greg's approach is to prepare simple and clean Italian food, "stuff like your Italian grandmother would make," including meatballs and Sunday sauce. He says his menu focuses less on proteins (you can visit his restaurant Cioppino for those) and more on fresh pastas, pizzas, sandwiches, and antipasti. One of the menu's showstoppers is the light and fluffy pillows of gnocchi served with a simple house-made sweet red sauce and sprinkled elegantly with Parmigiano Reggiano cheese.

After high school, Greg graduated from The Culinary Institute of America in Hyde Park, New York, and bounced around kitchens both in Pittsburgh and in New York City, even opening up his own restaurant right outside of Manhattan in New Jersey, before permanently returning to Pittsburgh. Back home, Greg served as the executive chef at the Steelhead Grill inside the Marriott City Center Downtown and helped the Big Burrito Group open Eleven in the Strip District.

When not at Osteria 2350 or at his two other restaurants, the aforementioned Cioppino and his downtown haunt Osteria 100, Greg can be found on his old country farmhouse, tending to his large garden. Right now, he says he doesn't have a lot of time to put into it, but eventually he wants to make it bigger and hopes to sell fresh produce to his restaurants and others around the city.

Osteria Meatballs

MAKES 20 MEATBALLS

3 slices bread
½ cup milk
1 large onion, cut into small dice
Extra-virgin olive oil
2 cups shredded mozzarella cheese
1 cup grated Parmigiano Reggiano
3 tablespoons salt
1 tablespoon pepper
1 tablespoon chopped parsley
5 pounds ground beef

To prepare the milk-soaked bread: In a bowl, place 3 slices of your choice of bread, torn into small pieces, and cover with about ½ cup of milk, enough to produce 1 cup of milk-soaked bread.

To prepare the meatballs: Preheat oven 500°F.

In a saucepan over medium heat, sweat the onion in a light drizzle of extra-virgin olive oil until soft and translucent. Let cool completely.

In a mixing bowl, add all ingredients, including the milk-soaked bread, to the ground beef and mix until incorporated. Scoop the mixture into ½-cup balls and place on a greased baking sheet, about 1 inch apart.

Bake for 10 minutes or until brown. Finish cooking meatballs in your favorite tomato sauce.

Paris 66

6018 Penn Circle South
Pittsburgh, PA 15206
(412) 404-8166
paris66bistro.com
Owners: Frederic and Lori Rongier
Master French Pastry Chef: David Piquard

Paris meets Pittsburgh at Paris 66 in the city's East End. Rather than two divergent cultures colliding, they do a bit of a tango with one another, each unique cuisine vying for attention yet somehow working harmoniously to create a sexy sampling of perfectly paired plates.

Frederic, a French native, and his wife, Lori, a western Pennsylvania native, help patrons fall in love with French cuisine through their accessible offerings, charming dining space and patio, and exquisitely displayed pastries.

Paris 66 is named for the true merging of two completely different worlds. The *66* tailing Paris in the nomenclature, reminiscent of the *66* tailing America's most famous roadway, Route 66, is no coincidence. Fred's desire to settle down and immerse himself in the United States has been a driving factor behind the restaurant.

Years ago, he aimed to introduce a new style of food to the area, that being French

food that everyone could enjoy, every day. He wanted there to be a plateful of food set upon the meticulously collaged tabletops, adorned with photograph and postcard relics from days gone by, and he wanted that food to appeal to the masses.

They have evolved, like all good restaurants do, to meet the growing demands of those who dine at Paris 66. What began as a cafe serving must-haves like the croque monsieur, crepes, and quiche is now a full-service restaurant specializing in unique fusion dishes utilizing ingredients from local farms.

Whether you take in the famous eggs Provençal, crepe with berry compote, pain au chocolat, and free-trade coffee at brunch on the back patio; enjoy a romantic dinner of *moules et frites;* or simply stop in for a few delicate pistachio *macarons,* you're sure to notice the way these innovative individuals have teamed up to reinvent the way people think about French food.

CRÈME BRÛLÉE

MAKES 15 RAMEKINS

10 grams liquid vanilla extract

1 liter plus 50 milliliters heavy cream

375 milliliters milk

20 egg yolks

225 grams sugar, plus additional sugar for serving

Special equipment:

Metric kitchen scale

Ramekins

Butane torch

In a saucepan, bring vanilla, heavy cream, and milk to a boil. In separate bowl, mix egg yolks and sugar until light and fluffy. Add the vanilla, cream, and milk mixture to the egg yolk and sugar mixture and blend until incorporated. Let mixture set, covered, for 12 hours in the refrigerator.

Preheat oven to 205°F.

Put the mixture in 15 individual ramekins. Bake in a water bath for 1 hour.

To serve: Sprinkle sugar on top of each ramekin. Caramelize with butane torch. Enjoy!

MUSSELS MARINIÈRE

SERVES 1 AS A MEAL OR 2 AS AN APPETIZER

1 pound Prince Edward Island mussels

1 teaspoon grapeseed oil

1 tablespoon diced shallot

1 tablespoon peeled and thinly sliced garlic

½ cup white wine

1 tablespoon butter

2 tablespoons minced parsley

⅛ cup fresh-squeezed lemon juice

Wash and remove the beards from the mussels.

Heat the oil in a 4-quart pot. Lightly sauté the shallot and garlic. Add wine and boil for 1 minute. Add cleaned mussels and boil on high heat for 2 minutes or until they begin to open. Remove from heat and leave covered for 2 additional minutes.

Place mussels in a large bowl and strain the broth into a clean saucepan. Add butter, parsley, and lemon juice, stirring until incorporated. Pour over mussels and serve with frites!

Frisée au Lardons

SERVES 4

1 cup 1-inch cubes of coarse country bread

1½ tablespoons extra-virgin olive oil

Salt and freshly ground pepper to taste

¾ pound thick-cut bacon, cut into ½-inch pieces

2 shallots, finely chopped

5 tablespoons red wine vinegar

6 cups water

1 teaspoon salt

1 teaspoon white wine vinegar

4 eggs

2 heads frisée, cored and leaves
    torn into 3-inch pieces

Preheat oven to 350°F.

Spread the bread cubes on a baking sheet. Sprinkle them with the olive oil and season with salt and pepper. Toast in the oven, turning once or twice, until golden, about 15 minutes. Set aside.

In a fry pan over medium-high heat, sauté the bacon, stirring occasionally, until crisp, about 4 to 5 minutes. Add the shallots and sauté until softened, about 1 minute. Add the red wine vinegar, reduce the heat to medium, and simmer

until slightly thickened, about 1 minute more. Season to taste with salt and pepper. Set aside and keep warm.

Pour 6 cups water into a large, deep fry pan or wide saucepan and add 1 teaspoon salt and the white wine vinegar. Bring to a simmer over high heat. Reduce the heat to medium to maintain a gentle simmer. Break 1 egg into a ramekin and slide it carefully into the simmering water. Working quickly, repeat with the remaining 3 eggs. Carefully spoon the simmering water over the

eggs until the whites are just opaque and firm and the yolks are still soft, about 3 minutes. Using a slotted spoon, transfer the eggs to a plate and set aside.

In a large salad bowl, combine the croutons and the frisée. Pour the warm dressing with the bacon pieces over the salad and toss to coat evenly. Divide the salad among shallow individual bowls, making sure there is an equal amount of bacon in each serving. Place a poached egg on top of each salad and serve immediately.

GABY ET JULES

PATISSERIES ET MACARONS
5837 FORBES AVENUE
PITTSBURGH, PA 15217
GABYETJULES.COM
(412) 682-1966

Squirrel Hill is dotted with many a hidden gem. Passersby can mosey along Murray and Forbes Avenues, taking pause at a world-famous record shop, an independent movie theater, and a French patisserie. If the scent of freshly baked *macarons* doesn't draw you into Gaby et Jules, the Parisian cafe-style seating along the narrow sidewalk will certainly catch your attention.

Owners Frederic and Lori Rongier and co-owner and Master French Pastry Chef David Piquard realized the need for a bakery in the neighborhood and, much to the delight of locals, planted down a quaint shop complete with drool-worthy display cases as far as the eye can see.

Gaby et Jules, named for Frederic's and David's grandfathers who always dreamed of owning a bakery, features beautifully prepared French artisan pastries and tarts, both the mini variety and larger size for much hungrier patrons, and, of course, David's famous *macarons*. Each delicacy, made with love, is a testament to the dedication David has for creating traditional desserts and presenting them in the most beautiful manner possible.

Indulge in éclairs, cry tears of joy over the flaky croissants, and eat your weight in fresh-baked bread, all in one place. Two men's dream of owning a bakery has become a reality for their grandsons and is a welcome addition to the upper end of Forbes Avenue.

PGH Taco Truck

(412) 841-9234
PGHTACOTRUCK.COM
OWNER: JAMES RICH

James Rich doesn't consider himself a chef, though he has the résumé and skills to prove otherwise. He simply considers himself a man who has eaten a lot of food and knows what tastes good. And what tastes good to him are tacos. Tons of tacos. His love of tacos began at fifteen on a trip to Mexico City with his grandmother. With his weekly allowance of about twenty dollars in his pocket, he snuck out of his hotel to an open-air market and purchased all the tacos he could. Six tacos to be exact. "I remember thinking, 'Wow, these are really good and really cheap,'" says James. "I immediately fell in love with them there."

Back in the States and during his time in college at Ohio University, James got his first taste of the mobile food business while working inside The Burrito Buggy, a food truck dishing out Americanized burritos. Despite the fact that he went home every night smelling like a burrito, he says he really fell in love with connecting with the people through that window.

Over twenty years later, James is connecting with customers through the window of the PGH Taco Truck. You aren't going to find any sad-tasting tacos on the truck's daily menu. James is a big fan of ethnic foods, such as Korean and Indian cuisines, and he incorporates these bold flavors into his tacos. An Indian butter-chicken taco with chile

yogurt and the Korean barbecue steak taco with truck-made kimchee can be found along with a curried organic potato taco with Sriracha cream and a pork taco with pineapple citrus salsa.

During the PGH Taco Truck's appearances around town, Pittsburghers often wait in lines for hours, sometimes even in the snow, for James's creations. "The fact that someone is willing to wait that long in those conditions for my food motivates me to wake up earlier, shop for different foods, and try more things on the truck."

Juicy Pork Tacos with Mango Jalapeño Salsa

MAKES 10 TACOS

2 pounds boneless pork shoulder

Sea salt and freshly cracked black pepper to taste

2 red onions, peeled and diced

6 fresh jalapeños

1 bunch fresh cilantro leaves, plus additional for serving

6 tablespoons olive oil

1 quart half-and-half, to cover the pork

Juice of 6 limes

1 tablespoon sea salt, or to taste

1 tablespoon cane sugar, or to taste

2 mangos, peeled and diced

Corn tortillas

Canola oil, rendered pork fat, or clarified butter,
    for cooking

Lime wedges

Fresh avocado, peeled and sliced

Special equipment:

Cast iron skillet (optional)

Meat thermometer

To prepare pork: Trim and cut pork shoulder into bite-size pieces, removing any silver skin and large pieces of fat. Rub the pork pieces with sea salt and freshly cracked black pepper to taste.

Place equal amounts of diced red onion into two small dishes. Clean fresh jalapeños, removing the seeds and veins. Add equal amounts into the bowls with the onions. Clean, dry, and chop a bunch of fresh cilantro, adding even amounts into both of the bowls with the onions and jalapeños.

Place pieces of pork into a ceramic bowl and mix in the contents of one of the bowls of chopped ingredients; reserve the second bowl for the salsa. Add 6 tablespoons olive oil and mix until combined. Cover the bowl with plastic wrap and let it rest in refrigerator for 1 hour.

After 1 hour, pull pork out of refrigerator and stir. Pour half-and-half into the bowl until pork is completely covered. Push the pork down into the bowl to completely cover with half-and-half. Re-cover the bowl with plastic wrap, place in refrigerator, and leave to marinate overnight.

To prepare the salsa: Into the second bowl of prepared ingredients, add the juice of 6 limes. Stir in 1 tablespoon each of sea salt and cane sugar. (More or less can be added depending on your taste). Cover bowl with plastic wrap and refrigerate overnight.

To finish the pork and salsa: The next day, after pork and salsa have marinated overnight, stir in 2 diced mangos to the salsa base. Add salt and pepper to taste.

To serve: Warm up stacked pairs of corn tortillas on a hot cast iron skillet (or nonstick griddle) until they start to blister. (Griddle temperature should be around 400°F.) After blistering, flip over and repeat on other side. They should be firm and not burnt.

Drain the marinade from the pork and place the pork on a tray lined with paper towels. Place small amounts of the pork into a hot skillet with canola oil (rendered pork fat or clarified butter will also work). Stir fry until golden brown. (The internal temperature of the pork should be around 145°F). Spoon the cooked pork into tortillas and top with salsa. Garnish with fresh cilantro, lime, and avocado slices.

Note from the chef: Mangos can be really fickle to clean depending on how ripe they are. Find fresh, precleaned, and sliced mango at your local grocery store. Canned mango is not preferred for this recipe; if you cannot find fresh mango, you may substitute fresh pineapple instead, which is also delicious. Please note that this recipe needs to be started a day in advance before you plan to serve.

PICCOLO FORNO

3801 BUTLER STREET
PITTSBURGH, PA 15201
(412) 622-0111
PICCOLO-FORNO.COM
CHEF/OWNER: DOMENIC BRANDUZZI

Domenic Branduzzi is about as Italian as they come. As well he should be, seeing how he was born in the Tuscan village of Lucca, Italy. He moved with his family to Pittsburgh when he was just a wee tyke, all of four years old, and began a life in the 'Burgh as the son of two talented individuals. He credits his father, a baker, and his mother, a cook, as his teachers, his inspiration, and his partners.

He grew up learning from them both while they ran Il Piccolo Forno, a small bakery in Pittsburgh's historic Strip District. Throughout the 1990s he helped his parents at their shop and spent summers back in Italy, eating epic meals with his family and learning to cook the traditional Tuscan dishes he loved so much.

Domenic lost his father and mentor shortly after he opened his very own restaurant, aptly named Piccolo Forno in the city's Lawrenceville neighborhood. In 2008, his mother joined him, and since then they have been putting together true Italian food like they remember eating in Italy.

You can taste the love Domenic has for his heritage in every dish he creates. From the house-made pastas to the wood-fired pizzas and gelato, everything served at Piccolo Forno hails from northern Italy. Says Domenic, "There's a place for meatballs, but it isn't in Tuscany, and it isn't at Piccolo Forno." Instead you'll enjoy dishes made with fresh, seasonal ingredients and a whole lotta passion. Also featured on the menu are traditional Tuscan meats like boar and rabbit.

These recipes, once unfamiliar to Pittsburghers, have made their way into the regular restaurant rotations for locals. By pairing such meats with homemade noodles and sauces and challenging their taste buds, Domenic has successfully trained his community to appreciate his style of cooking. He has in fact created a little piece of Italy right in the heart of Pittsburgh.

SUGO DI CINGIALE

BOAR RAGÙ

SERVES 6–8

For the bouquet garni:

1 tablespoon whole juniper berries
5 whole cloves
1 tablespoon whole fennel seeds
5 whole allspice berries
Cheesecloth, to wrap and tie ingredients

For the boar ragù:

Extra-virgin olive oil
3 pounds ground boar meat
Salt and pepper to taste
1 cup red wine (Chianti preferred)
2 carrots, peeled and finely chopped
2 celery stalks, finely chopped
2 shallots, chopped fine
2 garlic cloves, peeled and finely chopped
2 bay leaves
1 (6-ounce) can tomato paste
4 cups beef broth, plus additional as needed
1 teaspoon ground nutmeg
1 tablespoon bittersweet cocoa

6–8 servings cooked pasta of your choice

To prepare the bouquet garni: Place the juniper berries, cloves, fennel seeds, and allspice into a piece of cheesecloth. Knot the cheesecloth so the ingredients are unable to escape.

To prepare the boar ragù: In a heavy-bottomed saucepan, heat a film of oil over high heat. Add ground boar meat. Break up the meat while cooking. Season the meat with salt and pepper to taste and cook for 20 to 25 minutes.

Deglaze the pan with wine to pick up all the bits from the pan. Allow the alcohol to cook out. Add the carrots, celery, shallots, garlic, and bay leaves. Lower heat to medium-high, and cook until vegetables are soft, about 15 to 20 minutes. Add the tomato paste, beef broth, nutmeg, and cocoa, along with the bouquet garni. Simmer on medium-low heat for 45 to 60 minutes, stirring occasionally. Add more salt and pepper if desired. If the sauce gets too dry too fast, add more beef broth. Before serving with your desired pasta, make sure to remove the bouquet and the bay leaves.

Butternut Squash Risotto with Pancetta

SERVES 8

For the butternut squash:

1 medium-size butternut squash
Extra-virgin olive oil
Salt and pepper to taste
Chicken broth, as needed

For the pancetta:

Extra-virgin olive oil for sautéing
1 pound pancetta, cubed small

For the risotto:

1 yellow onion, peeled and diced
2 tablespoons chopped fresh rosemary
2 pounds arborio rice
1 cup dry white wine
12 cups chicken broth, warmed
2 tablespoons chopped fresh sage
2 cups grated Romano cheese

Special equipment:

Blender
Parchment paper

To prepare the butternut squash: Preheat oven to 375°F.

Cut the squash in half lengthwise and remove the seeds. Drizzle the inside of one half with oil, salt, and pepper. Place face down on a parchment paper–lined baking sheet or pan.

Peel and dice the second squash half into ½-inch cubes. Place on a separate oiled baking pan and sprinkle with salt, pepper, and another drizzle of oil. Bake the half and the cubes of squash in an oven for 30 minutes. Check and stir cubes periodically. The halved squash will be soft and the cubes, golden brown.

Once cooked, remove the squash from the oven. Peel and puree the halved squash; use some broth to help with this process if necessary.

To prepare pancetta: In a heavy-bottomed saucepan or dutch oven, heat a thin film of oil over medium-high heat. Add the pancetta pieces and cook until crispy, about 10 to 15 minutes. Once crisp, remove pieces from the pan and place them in a bowl to be used later; reserve the pan with the rendered fat.

To prepare the risotto: Add diced onions and rosemary to the still-hot pan of rendered pancetta fat. Cook until very soft and caramelized, about 10 minutes. Add the rice to the onions. Stir together, making sure all the rice gets toasted and coated with the rendered fat in the pan. Before the rice begins to stick, add white wine to deglaze the pan. Stir well and allow the alcohol to cook off. Once absorbed, add some of the heated broth, just enough to cover the rice. Lower the heat to medium and continue to stir. Once liquid is absorbed, add more broth, sage, and squash puree. Continue stirring and adding broth, a ladle at a time.

Add the squash cubes, pancetta, and Romano cheese to finish. Total cooking time for rice is 30 to 45 minutes; the rice should be soft but still al dente. Risotto should be more creamy and moist rather than sticky and dry. It is all right not to use all the broth.

PIPER'S PUB

1828 EAST CARSON STREET
PITTSBURGH, PA 15203
(412) 381-2797
PIPERSPUB.COM
OWNER: ANDREW TOPPING

At Piper's Pub in the South Side, European football games fill the television screens and fare from across the pond fills the plates. For over fifteen years, this bar and restaurant has been giving Pittsburghers a taste of the British Isles. Owner Andrew Topping says the success is simple: "We make really good food, and people like it."

In the late 1990s, thirty-year-old Andrew saw his career selling cigarette vending machines disappearing. But it was during his vending career that he developed a lot of relationships with many bar and restaurant owners, learning the ways of the industry. So when a shift in careers was upon him, he thought it was time to get into the business himself. Originally Andrew found a space for his bar in South Oakland, but he didn't quite pull the trigger. It was a chance run-in with an old friend in Squirrel Hill that led him to a spot for sale in the South Side. After viewing the property, Andrew immediately thought it would make a perfect pub.

Piper's Pub is a Scottish pub in honor of Andrew's off-the-boat Scottish grandfather, who passed away when Andrew was fourteen years old. The menu is filled with traditional fare from the British Isles, including stews, bangers and mash, and many variations of shepherd's pie. Bangers are sourced locally from Parma Sausage Products Inc. in the Strip, and beans are directly imported from the United Kingdom. Though keeping with the tradition of making really hearty meals, some of the menu items at Piper's aren't made according to traditional recipes. And when customers ask Andrew about straying from tradition, he is quick to say, "Your grandmother never worked here."

THE PUB CHIP SHOP

1830 EAST CARSON STREET
PITTSBURGH, PA 15203
(412) 381-2447
THEPUBCHIPSHOP.COM

Andrew Topping has made many trips to the United Kingdom since opening Piper's Pub, one of which sparked an idea for The Pub Chip Shop, located directly next door to Piper's. During the Queen's Diamond Jubilee in the summer of 2012, Andrew was in a district outside of Newcastle, England, in the wee hours of the morning and saw chip shops get pounded with customers in line for tasty street food after a long night of drinking. He immediately knew he could do the same thing back in Pittsburgh. "Piper's doesn't touch the late-night crowds looking to grab a quick bite to eat," says Andrew. "I can be on that level with really good food." And really good food there is. The Pub Chip Shop combines a butcher shop and chip shop in one, serving fish-and-chips, savory meat pies, sausage rolls, and other scratch-made street food from the United Kingdom to the late-night crowds in the South Side.

CRACKED BLACK PEPPER SEARED SALMON
WITH IRISH WHISKEY CREAM SAUCE

SERVES 4

For the salmon:

2 tablespoons cooking oil

4 (6-ounce) salmon fillets

Freshly cracked black pepper to taste

Sea salt to taste

For the Irish whiskey cream sauce:

½ cup finely diced Spanish onion

½ cup whiskey

2 tablespoons honey

½ cup chicken stock

1 cup heavy cream

1 teaspoon chopped fresh chives

1 teaspoon chopped fresh parsley

To prepare the salmon: Add cooking oil to a hot skillet.

Sprinkle salmon fillets with freshly cracked black pepper and sea salt. Place salmon in the hot skillet with the cooking oil and sear both sides for 2 minutes each. Reduce heat and cook for another 3 minutes per side. Set aside and keep warm while you prepare the Irish whiskey cream sauce.

To prepare the Irish whiskey cream sauce: In the skillet that the salmon was cooked in, add finely diced Spanish onion and caramelize. Deglaze the pan with whiskey and honey, cooking until the liquid is almost reduced. Add chicken stock and heavy cream. Reduce to thicken slightly, then strain. Add chopped fresh chives and parsley.

To serve: Piper's Pub suggests serving this dish with roasted root vegetables and whipped garlic mashed potatoes.

POINT BRUGGE CAFÉ

401 HASTINGS STREET
PITTSBURGH, PA 15206
(412) 441-3334
POINTBRUGGE.COM
EXECUTIVE CHEF: JAMES McCASLIN

You won't find Executive Chef James McCaslin and the three guys who man the Sunday brunch line at Point Brugge Café at the restaurant on Monday. No. Monday is for the open road. The four men ride their motorcycles (James rocks a thirty-year-old Kawasaki cruiser) to the Laurel Highlands and beyond. "We haven't decided on a name for our group," James laughs. "But that is just the way it is here. We are like a family."

Point Brugge Café is a bistro with European flair and a penchant for making every patron feel like part of the family. "We are a neighborhood place, first and foremost," says James. "We concentrate on simple food, prepared well, and served in a great atmosphere."

The cozy restaurant has a menu focused on Belgian cuisine. It features dishes like a hearty *carbonnade flamande,* which is braised beef with *frites,* and a mustard-crusted

salmon. And, awesomely, the bar carries a large selection of Belgian craft beers to complement the cuisine. The menu rotates four to five times per year, but one item never disappears: mussels. These mollusks are the true star here, with hundreds of pounds of the seafood eaten each week. The mussels are sourced directly from Prince Edward Island, twice per week, making the freshness palpable.

James came to Pittsburgh in 2002 for school and quickly found his passion for cooking. Making meals for friends in college provided a creative outlet and free food in exchange for the service. "When you are broke in college, that is a good way to eat," he says. "The entire point of cooking is to make people happy, and I fell in love with that."

Love, just like the mussels, isn't in short supply at Point Brugge Café, from the familial staff to the comforting Belgian fare. The only thing in short supply? Line cooks and chefs on Monday. You'll find those dudes on their hogs in the hills.

CARBONNADE FLAMANDE

SERVES 8

4 pounds beef chuck tenders
Salt and pepper to taste
Vegetable oil for cooking
1 onion, sliced
½ cup (1 stick) unsalted butter
½ cup all-purpose flour
2 teaspoons beef base
1 (12-ounce) bottle lager beer
1 (12-ounce) bottle brown ale
2 teaspoons light brown sugar
¼ pound dried cherries
¼ pound dried apricots, chopped
4 sprigs fresh rosemary, for garnish

Preheat oven to 400°F.

To prepare beef: Slice the beef into strips across the grain. The strips should be approximately 2 x 1 x ¼ inch. Place the strips into a perforated pan and allow the meat to rest for 10 minutes. Season the beef strips with salt and pepper.

As the beef is resting, ready a large sauté pan by adding vegetable oil and placing on medium-high heat, to sear the strips.

Place the seasoned beef in the sauté pan to sear. Due to the volume of beef, you may need to prepare separate batches. Transfer the seared beef to another large pan for braising.

To prepare the onions: In the same sauté pan used for searing the beef strips, sauté the sliced onion in a coating of oil. Add the sautéed onions to the beef.

To prepare roux: Using the same sauté pan, melt the butter. Stir in flour to make a roux. When the roux turns light brown, whisk in the beef base.

Add both beers to the sauté pan. Whisk to combine the beer with the roux and bring the mixture to a simmer. Once the roux mixture has been brought to a simmer, pour it into the beef pan. Add the brown sugar, dried cherries, and apricots to the beef pan as well.

Tightly cover the pan and braise in the 400°F oven for 3 hours.

Garnish with sprigs of rosemary and enjoy.

RED CURRY MUSSELS

SERVES 1–2

This recipe serves one as a light meal or two as an appetizer; larger amounts can be cooked in a larger dutch oven or stockpot. Remember to leave enough room to stir the mussels as they cook and open up.

For curry sauce:

1½ tablespoons peeled and minced ginger

1 tablespoon finely chopped shallots

Vegetable oil for cooking

2½–3 tablespoons red curry paste, to taste

1¼ teaspoons curry powder

3 tablespoons light brown sugar

1 tablespoon fish sauce

Juice of 1 lime

1 (14-ounce) can coconut milk

1⅓ cups heavy cream

For mussels:

1 pound mussels (about 18–24), cleaned

1 tablespoon minced garlic

2 tablespoons minced shallots

Vegetable oil for cooking

¾ cup dry white wine

½–¾ cup curry sauce (see above)

Few sprigs of fresh cilantro

Few sprigs of fresh basil

Crusty French or Italian bread, for mopping up sauce

Special equipment:

Blender

To prepare the curry sauce: Sweat the ginger and shallots in vegetable oil until the shallots are translucent. Add the curry paste and the curry powder to the ginger and shallots. Stir the mixture over medium-low heat for 2 minutes. Add the brown sugar and stir until it dissolves. Add fish sauce and bring to a simmer.

Place the curry mixture in the bowl of a blender, add lime juice, coconut milk, and heavy cream. Blend thoroughly.

Put mixture in an airtight container and store in the refrigerator until ready to use.

To prepare the mussels: Heat a sauté pan over medium-high heat. Cook the mussels, garlic, and shallots in a small amount of vegetable oil, stirring frequently, until garlic and shallots are aromatic and the first few mussels begin to open. Add wine; bring the wine to a boil.

Cover and steam for 5 to 7 minutes or until the mussels are open and the meat has pulled away from the sides of the shell. The meat should be firm to the touch.

Add the curry sauce. Bring to a boil and cook just until the sauce begins to thicken but still remains brothy. The sauce should be just thick enough to coat the shells of the mussels; add a little water if the sauce has become too thick. Toss the mussels with cilantro and basil if desired.

To serve: Serve mussels with crusty bread for mopping up the flavorful sauce.

Note from the chef: Curry paste can be found at Asian specialty stores. Point Brugge uses Mae Ploy brand. Most brands have similar flavor, but the spiciness varies widely. Coconut milk can be found at Asian speciality stores. Point Brugge uses Chaokah brand.

TIPS FOR CHOOSING AND CLEANING MUSSELS

From our friends at Point Brugge Café

Buy Prince Edward Island mussels if possible; they tend to be sweeter and slightly meatier.

Clean the mussels in a sink under cold running water. Discard any mussels that do not close when tapped or squeezed; then, pull any "beards" off (the beard is what mussels use to attach to rocks, rope, etc., and is a little clump of hairs that stick out from the crack in the side of the mussel shell). Scrub the mussels lightly with your hands, or a vegetable brush if they are excessively dirty (this is usually unnecessary).

Cleaning and prepping the mussels can be done a few hours or even a day before you intend to prepare them for eating. The mussels can be stored in the refrigerator, covered with a damp towel.

THE PORCH AT SCHENLEY

221 SCHENLEY DRIVE
PITTSBURGH, PA 15213
(412) 687-6724
THEPORCHATSCHENLEY.COM
CHEF: KEVIN HERMANN

It is easy to notice the olive branches inked onto Chef Kevin Hermann's upper left arm. Those symbols for peace and togetherness echo in Kevin's culinary philosophy. "A good meal can make you forget about whatever is worrying you," he says. "It can give you peace of mind."

Kevin started off his career in the kitchen of his family's house, where he became quickly enamored with food. "When I was a kid, I just messed around with food," he laughs. "When everyone was at the house, usually I was put to work plating the deli tray." This interest parlayed into waiting tables before heading to culinary school in Kansas City and then graduating from the Culinary Institute of America in New York. After running a restaurant in Rhinebeck, New York, Kevin found himself in Pittsburgh.

At The Porch, everything created in Kevin's kitchen is from scratch. Even the bacon is made in-house. The process of curing and smoking pork belly takes time (at least six days), but the payoff is worth it. On Saturday and Sunday, this delicious meat is served in a cast iron skillet for brunch. If the thought of that sizzling pork doesn't lure you in, the oft-rotating menu of urban farm-to-table dishes will do the trick. The kitchen sources from local farmers for beef and produce. The Porch also sources directly from the roof. Kevin grows heirloom tomatoes, hot and mild peppers, zucchini, and herbs, among others items, in his rooftop garden. The garden even plays host to a colony of bees buzzing with honey potential. Menu items benefit from this attention to fresh ingredients and include stars like a fig jam, goat cheese, and black truffle pizza served on a baking sheet and seared scallops resting on a blend of baby root vegetables.

Kevin notices that the people of Pittsburgh care about their food source. "People are excited about food in Pittsburgh," he says. "The food scene is really evolving, and I'm glad to be a part of it."

CORN-BREAD SKILLET

MAKES 7 SKILLETS; EACH SKILLET SERVES 2, OR A VERY HUNGRY 1

2½ cups cornmeal

2½ cups high-gluten flour

¾ cup granulated sugar

¾ tablespoon kosher salt

¾ tablespoon baking powder

1 teaspoon baking soda

3 cups buttermilk

1¾ cups heavy cream

½ cup sour cream

1 whole egg

1 egg yolk

½ pound (2 sticks) unsalted butter, melted

Vegetable or canola oil for the skillet

Rock sugar, for sprinkling on top of corn bread (use as much or as little as you would like to achieve desired sweetness)

Special equipment:

A small 5- to 6-inch cast iron skillet

Preheat oven to 400°F.

Place the cast iron skillet in the oven as it preheats so the skillet also warms up as you prepare the corn bread.

Mix the cornmeal, flour, sugar, salt, baking powder, and baking soda together in a large bowl. Once dry ingredients are mixed together, add the buttermilk, cream, sour cream, egg, egg yolk, and butter. Use a hand mixer to mix the ingredients until uniform.

Remove the warmed skillet from the oven. Lightly oil the skillet with vegetable oil or canola and add 2 cups of mixture to the skillet. Sprinkle with rock sugar before placing in the oven.

Bake until golden brown on top for 8 to 10 minutes. Repeat with the remaining batter.

Moroccan Couscous &
Red Wine–Braised Lamb Shanks

SERVES 4–6

For the couscous:

1 pound couscous
½ cup olive oil
1½ cups small-diced Spanish onion
⅓ cup small-diced carrots
⅓ cup small-diced celery
1 tablespoon turmeric
1 teaspoon ground cumin
1 teaspoon ground cinnamon
2 tablespoons chopped dried apricots
2 tablespoons chopped dried cherries
2 tablespoons chopped dried raisins
¼ cup chopped toasted pistachios
2 tablespoons chopped fresh parsley
Dash of salt and pepper

For the lamb shanks:

Salt and pepper
6 lamb shanks
¼ cup olive oil
1 pound Spanish onions, chopped
1 cup chopped celery
1 cup chopped carrots
2 garlic heads, cut in half crosswise
8 bay leaves
2 tablespoons whole black peppercorns
1 cup tomato paste
2 quarts red wine
8 whole thyme sprigs
4 whole rosemary sprigs
3 quarts beef stock

To prepare the couscous: Place a large pan over medium heat on the stovetop. Pour the couscous into the pan. Toast the couscous, stirring occasionally, until the couscous turns a golden brown.

After the couscous is toasted, add olive oil, onions, carrots, and celery. Stir and allow the mixture to cook until it becomes translucent. Add enough water to cover the couscous. Bring the water to a light simmer, stirring occasionally. The couscous will absorb all of the water. Once the water has been absorbed, remove the cooked couscous from the heat.

Stir in the spices, making sure to coat all of the couscous. Add the dried fruit, pistachios, and parsley. Season with salt and pepper to taste. Allow the couscous to cool before serving.

To prepare the lamb shanks: Preheat oven to 325°F.

In a heavy-bottomed pot over medium-high heat, season and brown the lamb shanks in olive oil. When lamb shanks are golden to dark brown, remove them from the pot and set aside.

In the same pot, add chopped onions, celery, carrots, and garlic. Cook vegetables until caramelized. Add bay leaves, black peppercorns, and tomato paste, combining them thoroughly. Add red wine, thyme, and rosemary, and reduce the liquid by half. Add beef stock and place the lamb shanks back into the pot. Add enough water to cover the lamb shanks.

Cover pan with aluminum foil and bake for 3½ hours or until the lamb shanks are tender. Remove the pan from the oven and carefully remove the shanks from the braising liquid. Set aside. Strain the liquid and place into a separate pot to reduce by half.

Serve lamb shanks and reduced sauce immediately over couscous.

Note from the chef: You can refrigerate the lamb shanks for up to 5 days or freeze up to 30 days.

Root 174

1113 South Braddock Avenue
Pittsburgh, PA 15218
(412) 243-4348
root174.com
Chef/Owner: Keith Fuller
Owner: Patrick Bollinger

At Root 174, Keith Fuller's skills lie not only in his cooking techniques but also in his dance moves. In the kitchen prepping for dinner service, he can often be found dancing around to the pop beats of Ke$ha. He laughs that no knives are involved during these dance outbursts, but sometimes utensils are.

In 2011 Keith opened Root 174 in Regent Square after leaving his executive chef position at Six Penn Kitchen in Pittsburgh's Cultural District. "I decided I wanted to make no money, work my entire life, and say goodbye to all my savings," says Keith. At his intimate and romantic thirty-eight-seat restaurant, he crafts elegant plates of food often made from offal and waste meat, such as heart sausage, headcheese, and duck fries,

aka duck testicles. "They're a lot bigger than you think," snickers Keith. "They're the reason why ducks have so much swagger." In addition to his meaty creations, Keith's ever-changing international-fusion menu always includes a vegan appetizer, entree, and dessert. He firmly believes that there should always be an option for everyone to eat.

At age fourteen, Keith got his first job in a kitchen at a hash house and fell in love with the food, the people, the lingo, and everything else. In his dad's eyes, he was destined to be a polymer scientist, but Keith dropped out of college to pursue cooking . . . and video games. "I knew I was going to drop out anyway, so I started playing video games," says Keith. "*The Legend of Zelda* and *Tony Hawk's Pro Skater* came out at around the same time. It was a bad time for me."

Both his love of cooking and video games are evident in his tattoos. The words *Cook Grow* and *Game Nerd* appear across his knuckles and fingers. And maybe one day, there will be a tattoo professing his love for Ke$ha . . . over his heart.

VEGAN CHICKPEA CURRY WITH CRISPY TOFU

SERVES 4–6

For the tofu:

¼ cup cornstarch
Salt and pepper to taste
1 pound block extra-firm tofu, cut into large cubes
2 tablespoons canola oil

For the curry:

2 (15-ounce) cans chickpeas, drained
Zest and juice of 1 lemon
3 tablespoons curry powder
1 quart olive oil
1 small bunch thyme, tied with string
10 garlic cloves, thinly sliced
3 quarts cherry tomatoes
½ cup chopped fresh marjoram
½ cup chopped fresh cilantro, including stems
Salt and pepper to taste
1 teaspoon sherry vinegar
1 tablespoon yogurt or vegan sour cream
1–2 sliced serrano peppers, to taste, for garnish
½ cup crushed pistachios, for garnish

Special equipment:

Candy thermometer

Preheat oven to 350°F.

To prepare the tofu: In a bowl, combine cornstarch, salt, and pepper. Add in tofu and toss until the cubes are completely covered.

In a saucepan over medium heat on the stove, heat the oil and fry tofu until all sides are golden brown. Remove tofu from oil and place on a cooling rack.

To prepare the curry: In a mixing bowl, mix together chickpeas, lemon juice, lemon zest, and curry powder. Set aside.

In a pot, add oil and bundle of thyme and heat to 200°F, using a candy thermometer to measure the temperature. Once the temperature is reached, add the sliced garlic and cook until golden brown. Pull out the bunch of thyme and

add the cherry tomatoes. Steep the cherry tomatoes until softened. Remove from stove and strain the cherry tomatoes and garlic from the oil using a slotted spoon; reserve.

Add garlic and tomatoes to the mixing bowl with chickpeas. Add in ¼ cup of the steeped oil from the garlic and tomatoes. Fold in marjoram, cilantro, salt, and pepper.

Bake tofu for about 3 to 5 minutes until heated through completely. In a sauté pan over medium heat, heat the chickpeas; add sherry vinegar to brighten their flavor. If you have any yogurt or vegan sour cream on hand, add 1 tablespoon to the chickpea mixture to cream it out.

To serve: Place chickpeas on a plate and the tofu on top. Add sliced serrano peppers (to your heat linking) and garnish with a handful of crushed pistachios.

FLOURLESS CHOCOLATE CAKE WITH CHOCOLATE GANACHE & BEET ICE CREAM

SERVES 4

For the beet puree:

2 large beets
1 teaspoon salt

For the beet ice cream:

1 cup milk
1 cup cream
6 egg yolks
3 tablespoons honey
1 teaspoon vanilla extract
¼ cup sugar
½ cup beet puree

For the chocolate ganache:

2 cups heavy cream
10 ounces bittersweet chocolate, roughly chopped
¼ teaspoon salt

For the flourless chocolate cake:

3 ounces (¾ stick) unsalted butter
6 ounces semisweet chocolate, roughly chopped
¾ cup granulated sugar
1 tablespoon vanilla extract
½ cup dark cocoa powder
3 eggs
¼ teaspoon sea salt

Pinch of sea salt for serving
Fresh mint leaves for garnish
Cocoa powder for dusting

Special equipment:

Blender
Ice cream maker
Double boiler

To prepare beet puree: In a pot on the stove, simmer beets in water with salt until tender. Once tender, remove beet skins and discard. Dice beets and puree in a blender until smooth. Set aside.

To prepare beet ice cream: In a saucepan, bring milk and cream to a simmer. In a mixing bowl, place unbeaten egg yolks and honey. When milk and cream reach a simmer, pour the vanilla extract and sugar into the bowl with the egg yolks and honey and whisk until combined. Slowly add the milk and cream mixture into the bowl to temper. Once combined, add in beet puree and set aside, covered, in the refrigerator to cool. Once cool, place into ice cream maker to churn. Freeze.

To prepare the chocolate ganache: In a saucepan, bring heavy cream to a simmer. Pour in chocolate and stir until chocolate has melted completely. Add in salt. Refrigerate until ganache hardens to an icing-like texture.

To prepare the flourless chocolate cake: Preheat oven to 350°F. Grease a 9 x 9-inch pan.

Important: While the oven is heating, place a metal container with hot water into the oven, which will put moisture into the oven. Leave water bath in for the whole duration of baking.

Using a double boiler, place butter and semisweet chocolate in the upper pot and whisk until chocolate and butter are melted. Add sugar and whisk for another 1 to 2 minutes until sugar just starts to dissolve. Whisk in vanilla extract and dark cocoa powder and remove from heat. Using a spatula, fold in eggs, one at a time; fold in sea salt.

Pour cake mixture into a greased pan. Using a spatula, spread mixture out evenly. Place in oven and bake for about 15 minutes. The cake should look slightly undone but still have buoyancy when touched. If too wet, bake for another 5 minutes and repeat if necessary. It is important that the cake looks slightly underdone for a moister cake.

To serve: Cut cake into triangle shapes and place two triangles at the center of a small plate. Place a quenelle of ganache on top of one triangle. Sprinkle a pinch of sea salt on top of the ganache. Place a scoop of beet ice cream next to ganache. Garnish each serving with a single mint leaf and dusting of cocoa powder.

Salt of the Earth

5523 Penn Avenue
Pittsburgh, PA 15206
(412) 441-7258
saltpgh.com
Owner: Kevin Sousa

"If you feel like you could make what we serve you at home, then we've failed," says Kevin Sousa, owner and chef at Salt of the Earth. Kevin and his team, including Chef de Cuisine Chad Townsend, and the front-of-house staff, strive to make Salt an unrepeatable experience. He continues, "We are not typical farm-to-table. Our food is not simple; it is complex."

Sourcing from a farm within walking distance of the restaurant, Salt prepares eclectic dishes that change daily, and flavorful combinations that take diners off the beaten path. Even the cuts of meat are adventurous, as Kevin considers all parts of the animals served fair game—from pig's tail to beef tendon. The atmosphere at Salt is unique as well. The 125-year-old building features a large chalkboard menu, an open kitchen, and some communal dining. The long, oak tables, made from trees in Allegheny Cemetery that

fell during a storm, allow diners to sit with friends, both old and new.

While sometimes the food concepts are challenging, Kevin's philosophy is easy: "We just want to make really nice food and not take ourselves too seriously."

Kevin never actually wanted to be a chef. After working in his father's restaurant in McKees Rocks, he left western Pennsylvania and went to art school. To pay his way, he found himself working in kitchens again. "It just came natural," Kevin says. "It is a cliché, but the kitchen picks you."

He moved home to the Pittsburgh area, after attending culinary school, and worked in several restaurants before taking the leap to ownership. Salt opened in 2010. Kevin opened three more restaurants in the years that followed: Station Street Hot Dogs, Union Pig & Chicken, and Harvard & Highland.

Keeping his culinary empire thriving will take hard work. Lucky for Kevin, he has those two words tattooed on his hands. A reminder? Perhaps. A mantra? Absolutely.

Salmon—Cauliflower, Celery, Apple

SERVES 3

For the cauliflower milk:

1 large head cauliflower
946 milliliters heavy cream

For the cauliflower ice cream:

900 milliliters half-and-half
200 milliliters cauliflower milk (see above)
154 grams atomized glucose
0.44 gram iota carrageenan
2.2 grams Kelgum
6.6 grams dextrose

For the celery sheet:

800 milliliters celery juice
4 grams agar agar
8 grams sugar
14.4 grams powdered gelatin
12 grams kosher salt

1 pound raw salmon, medium diced
1 Fuji apple, diced into ⅛-inch pieces
Sea trout roe for garnish
Wild cress leaves and blossoms for garnish
Delicate celery leaves for garnish
Grapefruit supremes (just the flesh)
Lemon juice to taste
Chives, chopped
Sea salt to taste

Special equipment:

Metric kitchen scale
Thermometer
Chinois
Pacojet, or home ice cream maker
2 Pacojet canisters
3 quarter-sheet pans

To prepare the cauliflower milk: In a saucepan, boil the cauliflower head in heavy cream until tender. Once tender, strain the cream mixture and reserve liquid.

To prepare the cauliflower ice cream: On a stove top, combine half-and-half, cauliflower milk, glucose, iota carrageenan, Kelgum, and dextrose. Heat the mixture to 180°F. Once the temperature is reached, pass the mixture through a chinois into a bowl. Allow the mixture to chill.

Pour the mixture into two Pacojet canisters. Freeze. Pacotize. If using an ice cream maker, rather than a Pacojet, place mixture in ice cream maker to churn. Freeze.

For the celery sheet: On a stove top, combine the celery juice, agar agar, sugar, gelatin powder, and kosher salt. Bring the mixture to a boil. Pass through a chinois onto three quarter-sheet pans. Chill the pans.

To serve: Assemble salmon, apple, roe, wild cress, celery leaves, and grapefruit supremes on top of a celery sheet as pictured on previous page. Dress with lemon juice, chives, and sea salt.

Savoy

2623 Penn Avenue
Pittsburgh, PA 15222
(412) 281-0660
savoypgh.com
Owner: Chuck Sanders
Executive Chef: Kevin Watson

Prior to joining Savoy as executive chef, Kevin Watson's career was balling. He was both a personal chef and caterer to many of the Pittsburgh Steelers, cooking at their private parties and catering special athlete-inspired meals. And he was a chef instructor at a local culinary institute. So when approached to lead the kitchen at Savoy, he naturally turned down the job, telling the restaurant's owners, "I just can't fit that into my life." But after a few business meetings and some convincing by Savoy's owners, including the opportunity to write his own salary, he accepted the job. And hyperventilated.

At Savoy, Kevin's menu is swanky, sexy, and cool, just like the space itself. Inspirations of the contemporary American menu come from many types of cuisine, such as Mediterranean and Southern, but mostly they draw from Kevin's love for nostalgia. "I like to take foods we can relate to and twist them," says Kevin. And he does just that with his childhood comfort food, chicken and waffles. He remembers the best part of eating a fried chicken dinner from his youth was the bite he got when the sides of mashed potatoes and creamed corn ran together. Now with his modernized chicken and waffles dish, he accompanies the crispy chicken and fluffy waffle with a chipotle-spiced creamed-corn pudding.

Over twenty-five years ago, Kevin got his first job working in a kitchen with his cousin at a small, family-style restaurant in his hometown of Erie, Pennsylvania. Eager to test his cooking skills in a metropolitan city, Kevin headed for Pittsburgh and worked at a few local restaurants before attending culinary school in 1991. After culinary school, Kevin performed his externship at The Ritz-Carlton, Amelia Island, leaving the hotel as a pastry chef. Back in Pittsburgh at Savoy, Kevin is serious about his food. He keeps it simple and straightforward. "My theory is to stay out of the way and let the food speak for itself," says Kevin. "It's all about using premium products, applying the right technique, and seasoning to perfection."

ROASTED BUTTERNUT SQUASH CHOCOLATE RAVIOLI WITH LOBSTER BASIL CREAM SAUCE

SERVES 2

For the butternut squash ravioli filling:

1 butternut squash
Olive oil
Salt and pepper to taste
1 cup ricotta cheese
1 teaspoon to 1 tablespoon maple syrup to taste
Freshly ground white pepper to taste
3 tablespoons heavy cream
3 tablespoons grated Parmigiano Reggiano cheese
Pinch of nutmeg
1 tablespoon unsalted butter

For the pasta dough:

½ cup semolina flour
1½ cups all-purpose flour
2 tablespoons unsweetened cocoa powder
3 large eggs, lightly beaten
1 tablespoon olive oil
1 egg white, lightly beaten

For the lobster basil cream sauce:

2 cups heavy cream
2 (4-ounce) lobster tails
8-12 cooked butternut squash ravioli (see above)
2 teaspoons basil chiffonade
4 ounces grated Parmesan cheese

Special equipment:

Food processor
Pasta machine (optional)

To prepare the butternut squash ravioli filling: Preheat the oven to 400°F.

Split the butternut squash in half lengthwise and scoop out the seeds. Drizzle both halves with olive oil and sprinkle with salt and pepper. Bake on a rimmed sheet or in a baking dish for 30 to 40 minutes, or until soft. Be careful not to burn. Remove from oven and allow to cool. Once completely cooled, scoop out the roasted butternut squash flesh from the skin and place into a bowl. Mash with a fork. Add the ricotta cheese and drizzle maple syrup to taste into the bowl and mix. Add freshly ground white pepper, heavy cream, Parmigiano Reggiano cheese, and nutmeg. Mix until combined.

In a hot skillet on medium heat, swirl butter until melted. Continue cooking over medium heat. When foam subsides, the butter will start to turn golden brown as the natural sugars in the butter caramelize.

Place roasted butternut squash mixture and caramelized butter into a food processor and blend until smooth. Set aside.

To prepare pasta dough by hand: Add semolina flour, all-purpose flour, and unsweetened cocoa powder to a large bowl. Mix together with a fork until combined. Make a well in the center of the flour-cocoa mixture and add the lightly beaten eggs and oil. Mix with a fork until combined. The mixture should form a stiff dough. If needed, add 1 to 2 tablespoons of water to loosen the dough. On a floured surface, knead the dough for about 3 to 4 minutes. Wrap dough in plastic wrap and place in refrigerator for 30 minutes.

To prepare pasta dough using a food processor: Combine the eggs and oil in the bowl of the processor and blend. Add semolina flour and process until blended. Add all-purpose flour and blend. Add unsweetened cocoa powder and blend. If needed, add 1 to 2 tablespoons of water to loosen the dough. Wrap dough in plastic wrap and place in refrigerator for 30 minutes.

To prepare the ravioli: With a pasta machine on a #6 setting or using a rolling pin, roll out 12-inch-long sheets of dough to a ⅛-inch thickness. Cover sheets of dough that are not being used with a damp towel so they do not dry out.

Cut the 12-inch sheets of dough into 3-inch squares. Place 2 teaspoons of the roasted butternut squash filling into the center of each pasta square. Brush the beaten egg white around all four edges of the pasta square, fold over, and seal, forming a triangle. Be sure to completely seal each ravioli.

Add ravioli to a pot of salted, boiling water. Cook until al dente, about 2 to 3 minutes or until the ravioli float to the top of the water and are pale in color. Drain well.

To prepare the lobster basil cream sauce: Heat a sauté pan on medium heat until just warm. Add heavy cream and lobster tails and cook for 2 to 4 minutes. Add cooked ravioli and simmer for 2 more minutes. Turn off heat and add basil and Parmesan cheese.

To serve: Plate ravioli and top with lobster basil cream sauce.

Note from the chef: This recipe makes 24 ravioli. Once the ravioli are assembled, they can be frozen (uncooked) in a single layer and then transferred to freezer bags.

SEVICHE

930 PENN AVENUE
PITTSBURGH, PA 15222
(412) 697-3120
SEVICHE.COM
OWNER: YVES CARREAU
CHEF: CALEB LONGACRE

It's hard to picture Chef Caleb Longacre as ex-military with his cargo shorts, T-shirt, and knitted beanie in the dead of winter, almost walking on air as tickets for a certain comedic concert pass from his friend's hands into his. Nevertheless, he served our country in the army, spending time both in the United States and abroad sharpening the skills that have made him the chef he is today. His innocent smile lights up the restaurant, a tough task considering it is one of the brightest restaurant spaces in all of Pittsburgh.

Seviche, on Penn Avenue in the Cultural District Downtown, has been Caleb's home for several years. Here he's been concocting recipes and feeding the curious minds of western Pennsylvania's steel town. Seviche, aptly named for the dish of citrus-marinated raw fish, serves up food to meet the delights of anyone's taste buds. In addition to the Corn and Goat Cheese Croquettas, Asian tartare, and Cuban sushi roll, Caleb exercises his energetic imagination and often works overtime to create specialty menu items.

Well known for its elaborate and colorful happy hours, Seviche is also known, respected, and loved for its adaptable small plates and jovial atmosphere. It's a place where dancing is encouraged and sharing is a must. Its location in the heart of Downtown makes it the optimal place to grab a cocktail, before or after a show. It exudes excitement and a sense of exotic wonder, creating the perfect place for a first date.

With each passing day, Caleb and Seviche grow together and aim to please Pittsburghers' palates with plenty of new flavor combinations for meat eaters, vegetarians, and vegans alike. It's clear that this is a place to have fun with your food.

Mint & Mango Seviche with Salmon

SERVES 4–6

1 pound Scottish salmon, skin removed

Juice of 8 limes

2 tablespoons pomace oil or olive oil

1 red onion

2 jalapeño peppers

2 ripe mangos

½ tablespoon salt

¼ cup finely chopped cilantro

¼ cup finely chopped mint

Dice salmon into small cubes approximately 1 inch in size. Place in a large bowl.

Add the lime juice and pomace oil to the salmon. Marinate for 1 to 1½ hours in the refrigerator.

While the salmon is marinating, peel and dice the onion, and seed and dice the jalapeños and mangos. Add to the marinated fish mixture. Stir in salt, cilantro, and mint. Cover and place back in refrigerator for at least 30 minutes to allow flavors to mix.

Serve with triangles of warm corn tortillas.

SPOON

134 SOUTH HIGHLAND AVENUE
PITTSBURGH, PA 15206
(412) 362-6001
SPOONPGH.COM
CHEF/OWNER: BRIAN PEKARCIK
OWNER: RICHARD STERN

When Brian Pekarcik and his business partner, Richard Stern, were searching the city looking for the perfect location to open up Spoon, Brian never thought it would be in East Liberty. "Being back in Pittsburgh and not knowing about the revitalization happening in the neighborhood, I thought Rick was crazy," says Brian. But Rick wasn't crazy because East Liberty is "going off right now." The vibrant neighborhood is home to two of Brian's restaurants: Spoon, a casual/upscale American restaurant, and BRGR, Pittsburgh's first gourmet burger restaurant.

At Spoon, Brian is constantly changing his small dinner menu of hot and cold appetizers and entrees to keep things interesting, all of which maintain the farm-to-

table philosophy he firmly believes in. While working for one of the pioneers of this philosophy, Bradley Ogden in California, Brian was taught to source regionally, support local farms, and structure menus based off seasonality and availability. "It's not cliché to be farm-to-table," says Brian. "It's what I know."

After he sustained a baseball injury in college at John Carroll University, Brian's parents made him find a job. He started working at a greasy spoon–type place right off campus and fell in love with the business. After graduation, he moved to California and made it a point to work with some of the best chefs in the industry. Back home in Pittsburgh since 2010, he lights up when he talks about his colleagues here. "Keith Fuller, Richard DeShantz, Trevett Hooper, Justin Severino, and I go out together all the time. We are genuine friends who want the same thing: to make Pittsburgh a great culinary town. As business owners and chefs, we understand that it takes a collaborative movement to make things great." And their talents are definitely making things great!

AMERICAN-STYLE DIM SUM

CITRUS-GLAZED PORK BELLY BITES

SERVES 6–8

2 quarts orange juice
4 tablespoons minced ginger
4 tablespoons minced garlic
4 tablespoons minced green onions
½ cup soy sauce
¼ cup rice vinegar
1 (25-ounce) bottle sweet chili sauce
   (Mae Ploy preferred)
3 pounds pork butt

To prepare the sauce: In a saucepan over medium heat, add orange juice, ginger, garlic, green onions, soy sauce, and rice vinegar and reduce by three-quarters. Once reduced, add sweet chili sauce and simmer over low heat until the sauce is further reduced by half. Set aside to cool.

For the pork: Sear pork butt on high heat until heated through and crispy on all sides. Drain remaining fat in pan. Add enough sauce to coat the pork evenly.

To plate: Cut pork into medium-size pieces and serve in a bowl with chopsticks. Pork can also be served with soba noodles or in lettuce wraps.

Note from the chef: Confit pork belly can also be used in this recipe.

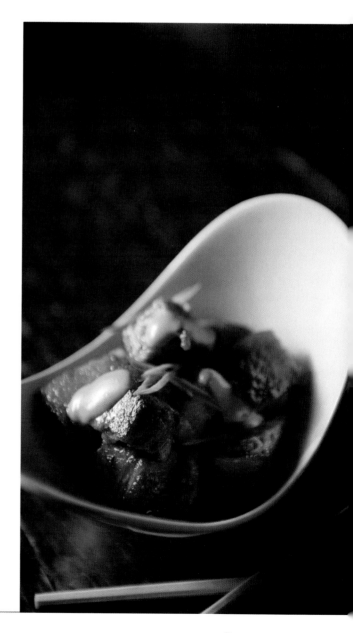

Gorgonzola Blue Cheese Soufflé with a Fall Orchard Salad

MAKES 4–6 RAMEKINS

For the soufflé:

2 ounces (½ stick) unsalted butter, plus additional for preparing the ramekins
6 tablespoons all-purpose flour, plus additional for preparing the ramekins
2 cups cold milk
7½ ounces Gorgonzola cheese
Salt and pepper to taste
8 egg yolks
8 egg whites

For the salad:

2 Granny Smith apples, cored and sliced
2 Honeycrisp, Gala, or Fuji apples, cored and sliced
2 Red Bartlett or Bosc pears, cored and sliced
2 large handfuls (or 1 small bag) Sylvetta or baby arugula
½ cup crumbled Gorgonzola cheese
½ cup candied walnuts
¼ cup balsamic vinaigrette (white balsamic vinaigrette preferred, but substitute dark balsamic vinaigrette if necessary)
Salt and pepper to taste

Special equipment:

Stand mixer
4–6 (4-ounce) ramekins

To prepare the soufflé: Preheat the oven to 300°F.

Melt the butter in a saucepan over medium heat. Add flour and stir rapidly with a wooden spoon, making a blond roux. Continue to cook for 2 minutes. Slowly add cold milk to make a béchamel, whisking constantly being careful not to burn. Cook for approximately 10 minutes over medium heat. Remove from heat and whisk in the Gorgonzola cheese. Season with salt and pepper to taste and let cool slightly. Add egg yolks one at a time, whisking each in. Cool mixture completely.

In the bowl of a stand mixer, whisk the egg whites to soft peaks. Fold half of the egg whites into the cheese mixture until completely incorporated. Fold in the remaining egg whites.

Butter and flour four to six 4-ounce ramekins. Divide the soufflé batter evenly among the ramekins and place them in a water bath. Bake for 15 to 18 minutes until light golden brown. Remove from molds.

To prepare the salad: Combine the sliced apples, pears, arugula, Gorgonzola cheese, candied walnuts, and white balsamic vinaigrette in a bowl. Add additional vinaigrette if necessary. Season with salt and pepper to taste.

To serve: Arrange salad mix in the middle of a large platter and place warm soufflés around.

SQUARE CAFE

1137 SOUTH BRADDOCK AVENUE
PITTSBURGH, PA 15218
(412) 244-8002
SQUARE-CAFE.COM
OWNER: SHERREE GOLDSTEIN
CHEF: KEVIN KELLY

Sometimes life wants you to have breakfast for dinner. Square Cafe wants you to have dinner for breakfast. Short ribs, prosciutto, and ahi tuna are all things you can find incorporated into the breakfast fare at the vibrant little cafe in Regent Square.

Owner Sherree Goldstein opened Square Cafe ten years ago with a dream and no formal restaurant experience. "I thought I was going to build a little cafe with some good pastry and coffee, and it morphed into this whole other thing," says Sherree. "Now people come here for more than just coffee and eggs."

Small-batch coffee, specially roasted by Kiva Han Roasters (based out of Cranberry), produce that is locally sourced, and rotating artwork from up-and-coming artists are all part of what keep patrons coming back for more. And let's not forget about the food.

The seasonal menu is filled with inspiration from Sherree's travels around the country. "If I have a really great dinner, I try and figure out how I can make it an egg dish. Or if I have a dessert somewhere, we try and figure out how to make a pancake or french toast out of it."

One of the most popular menu items is the Veggie Overload Omelet. It comes jam-packed with sautéed vegetables like zucchini, squash, spinach, mushrooms, peppers—basically any vegetable you can think of. You can also toss in Gouda, Havarti, Amish cheddar, and more.

Other seasonal fan favorites include Green Eggs & Ham made with homemade pesto, brussels sprouts hash, and the ever-popular Hopple Popple, an egg, potato, mushroom, onion, bell pepper, spinach, ham, and cheese scramble. If you weren't a morning person before, you will be after one bite.

GREEN EGGS & HAM

SERVES 6

For the pesto:

½ pound basil
½ cup finely chopped garlic
½ cup grated Parmesan cheese
½ cup finely chopped pine nuts
Juice of ½ lemon
½ teaspoon salt
½ teaspoon pepper
Olive oil (usually about ½–1 cup)

For the green eggs & ham:

12 eggs
½ cup whole milk
½ cup pesto (see above)
2 pounds thick-cut ham, diced
1 cup grated mozzarella or provolone cheese

Toasted grain bread, for serving
Jam, for serving

Special equipment:

Food processor

To prepare the pesto: Clean and remove leaves from the basil. Place basil, garlic, Parmesan cheese, pine nuts, lemon juice, and salt and pepper into a food processor. Slowly add the olive oil until mixture until it reaches desired consistency. (It should be thick like a sauce).

To prepare green eggs and ham: Preheat oven to 450°F.

Crack eggs into large bowl. Whip eggs and milk together until well blended. Mix in pesto and ham.

Place a large nonstick, ovenproof pan on the stove burner and let the pan get warm. Slowly pour the mixture into the pan, scrambling while it cooks. When the eggs are just underdone layer the cheese on top and place the pan in oven for just a few minutes while the cheese warms.

To serve: Divide into equal parts and serve with a toasted grain bread and jam.

VEGAN BANANA-SPICE PANCAKES

SERVES 4

2 cups flour

⅓ cup light brown sugar

1 teaspoon baking powder

¼ teaspoon salt

4 tablespoons cinnamon

1 tablespoon vanilla extract

2 whole ripe bananas, smashed

8–12 ounces soy milk (depending on desired consistency)

Canola oil for cooking

Maple syrup for serving

In a large mixing bowl, hand mix the flour, brown sugar, baking powder, salt, cinnamon, vanilla, bananas, and soy milk.

Coat the bottom of a large, hot skillet with canola oil. Using a measuring cup, pour ½ cup batter into the skillet. Let the batter cook approximately 2 minutes on one side; batter will start to bubble and brown around the edges when ready to flip. Once flipped, let pancake set completely.

Note from the chef: Vegan banana-spice pancakes are best served with local maple syrup from *Paul Bunyan Sugar Camp* located in Somerset County.

STAGIONI

2104 EAST CARSON STREET
PITTSBURGH, PA 15203
(412) 586-4738
STAGIONIPGH.COM
CHEF/OWNER: STEPHEN FELDER
OWNER: CARA DELSIGNORE

Fresh mozzarella is all about texture. Typically, mozzarella curd is stretched in warm water, formed by hand, set in an ice bath, and refrigerated for use later. At Stagioni fresh mozzarella is delivered to your table mere moments after it's made—creamy, barely set, and still warm. It creates an unparalleled experience that will make it hard to go back to anything else. This same mindful attention and desire for quality goes into each dish Chef/Owner Stephen Felder plates at Stagioni.

Stephen stumbled into cooking. Starting out, he was influenced by his southern upbringing in North Carolina: the easy pace, simplicity of cooking, and of course, the rich flavors. He then graduated to Italian cuisine, picking up skills and know-how along the way before moving to Pittsburgh to open Stagioni with co-owner, Cara DelSignore.

Staying true to its translation (*stagioni* means "seasons" in Italian), Stephen decides what to feature on the menu by season. In colder months, the menu is reminiscent of fare found in northern Italy like polentas and braises. During warmer weather, the menu focuses on the southern region of Italy, incorporating tomatoes, eggplant, and peppers

into dishes. "We use Italian techniques but not necessarily the way that it's traditionally done," says Stephen. "We'll have *bagna càuda* (garlic, anchovy, butter, and olive oil) that we'll use as a sauce on a scallop dish, where traditionally you'd dip raw vegetables in it for a first course."

That same simple, seasonal philosophy is translated to the drink menu at Stagioni; Cara develops both the cocktail and wine list. She works with wine importers to offer unique yet familiar wines, develops cocktails to pair with the menu, and also tracks down hard-to-find Italian craft beers.

BRACIOLE

SERVES 4–6

For the steak:

1 (1½–2 pound) flank steak
½ pound prosciutto, thinly sliced
1 pound Grana Padano cheese, cut into
　　¼-inch batons
Vegetable oil
2 large Spanish onions, julienned
4 garlic cloves, minced
1 cup red wine
2 (28-ounce) cans whole peeled tomatoes,
　　drained and pulsed in food processor

1 pound dried pappardelle pasta

Special equipment:

Food processor
Meat mallet
Kitchen twine

To prepare the flank steak: Preheat oven to 375°F.

Trim the steak of any silver skin and large pieces of fat. Slice the meat into long, thin strips (a little thicker than ¼-inch), cutting against the grain of the meat and at the most acute angle possible.

Place a few strips of meat between two sheets of plastic wrap. Pound the meat with a meat mallet until uniform in thickness and about ¼-inch thick. Continue pounding out the rest of the meat.

Lay the meat out on a cutting board and cover with one slice of prosciutto, torn about the same size as the meat. Place one piece of Grana Padano on each piece and roll it up. Tie a small piece of kitchen twine around each roll to keep it together while cooking.

Heat a large, heavy-bottomed sauté pan over medium-high heat. Cover the bottom of the pan with a thin layer of oil and sear the beef until dark brown, then turn it over and sear the other side. Be sure to do this in small batches to keep the pan hot so the meat will continue to sear and not steam.

Transfer the meat to a casserole dish. Discard the leftover oil and, starting with fresh oil, sear the rest of the meat and transfer it to the casserole dish.

Add enough oil to cover the bottom of a pan and add the onions. Stir to coat the onions in the oil. When the onions become translucent, add garlic and cook for about 2 minutes. Add wine and use a spatula to scrape the brown bits off the bottom of the pan to deglaze. Bring to a boil and add tomatoes.

Pour onions, garlic, and tomatoes into the casserole dish with beef. Cover with foil and place in the oven for 1½ hours. The meat should be very tender but not falling apart. If it isn't quite tender, put it back into the oven. Remove meat from sauce and allow to rest for at least 20 minutes. Slice meat.

To prepare the pasta: Cook the pasta in heavily salted, boiling water. When the pasta is about 1 minute away from being done, drain it. Reserve about 1 cup of the pasta water.

Put the sauce in a large pot (big enough to hold the pasta and sauce). Cook the pasta in the sauce for a minute or so, adding a couple of splashes of pasta water if it is too thick. Add the remaining cheese to the pasta and stir.

To serve: Plate family style, with pasta in a large plate and braciole on a separate dish.

Szmidt's Old World Deli

509 Greenfield Avenue
Pittsburgh, PA 15207
(412) 904-3558
SZMIDTS.COM
Chef/Owner: Darren Smith

Darren Smith doesn't cut corners at his restaurant. He does everything the old-fashioned way: by hand. Bread, meat, sauces—all of it is made in-house from scratch. How'd his intense dedication to homemade start? Corned beef.

On a trip to New York City, he tried the corned beef from the famous Katz's Delicatessen. He was instantly hooked and determined to bring the quality and flavor back to Pittsburgh. He set up a makeshift chemistry lab and went to work perfecting the brine to corn his beef. Several months and thousands of dollars in meat later, Darren's mad-science experiment finally paid off.

After corned beef, Darren started making pierogies and then tackled pastrami. With each new recipe he developed, he got closer to making his childhood dream of opening a small restaurant a reality.

Darren opened Szmidt's Old World Deli (pronounced Szchmeeds) with the goal of creating homemade comfort food just like your old Polish grandma used to make. Only better. The extensive menu offers Darren's homemade corned beef, pastrami, roast beef, or turkey on a variety of homemade breads with a variety of sauces and toppings. There's also a large selection of salads, sides (try the thinly sliced cucumbers in candied white vinegar!), and let's not forget pierogies. Old World choices include potato and cheese and sauerkraut; New World choices include buffalo chicken, Reuben, and Thanksgiving; and sweet pierogies include Granny Smith apple and peanut butter cup.

Speedy Pierogies

Pierogies are tasty and, apparently, fast. The Pittsburgh Pirates have adopted these delicious treats as game-day mascots that compete in the Pierogy Race. The race features four speedy and carb-heavy competitors: Sauerkraut Saul, Cheese Chester, Jalapeño Hannah, and Oliver Onion. During every Pittsburgh Pirate game day, these filled-dough darlings race 280 yards around PNC Park after the fifth inning. Get your tickets to see the filled noodles race, and oh yeah, to see some baseball, at pirates.mlb.com.

Cashew Praline Bacon BLT

SERVES 2

1 pound thick-cut bacon
6 teaspoons light brown sugar
1 ounce pecan halves
1 ounce cashew halves
4 bread slices
Handful of lettuce
2 tomatoes, sliced
Roasted Garlic Mayonnaise (see page 180)

Special equipment:

Food processor

Preheat oven to 400°F.

Line a sheet pan with aluminum foil. Arrange the bacon in a single layer on a cooling rack and set it in the prepared sheet pan. Bake until the bacon browns and the fat is cooked to personal preference, about 30 to 35 minutes.

Combine brown sugar, pecans, and cashews in a food processor. Pulse about fifteen times or until the pecans and cashews and are finely chopped.

Remove the bacon from the oven and sprinkle with the brown sugar mixture, patting it down to adhere. Return to the oven and bake until the bacon is crisp, about 10 minutes.

Cool on the rack for 10 minutes before serving.

To serve: Grab slices of your favorite bread and lightly toast each slice. Place bacon, lettuce, and tomato slices on toasted bread and smear with Roasted Garlic Mayonnaise. Enjoy!

ROASTED GARLIC MAYONNAISE

MAKES 1 CUP

For the mayonnaise base:

1 large egg yolk, at room temperature
2 teaspoons lemon juice
1 teaspoon Dijon mustard
¼ teaspoon kosher salt
1 teaspoon cold water
¾ cup neutral oil (safflower or canola)

For roasted garlic mayonnaise:

12 garlic cloves
1 tablespoon vegetable oil
1 tablespoon fresh lemon juice
1 teaspoon Worcestershire sauce
1 cup mayonnaise base (see above)
¼ cup chopped fresh parsley
¼ cup chopped fresh basil
Salt and pepper to taste

Special equipment:

Blender

To prepare the mayonnaise base: In medium bowl, whisk together the egg yolk, lemon juice, mustard, salt, and cold water until the mixture is frothy. Whisking constantly, slowly drizzle in the oil until the mixture has a thick consistency. When the mayonnaise emulsifies and starts to thicken, you can add the oil in a thin stream, instead of drop by drop.

To prepare the roasted garlic mayonnaise: Preheat oven to 300°F.

Place garlic cloves and oil in small baking dish and stir well. Bake mixture for 30 minutes or until garlic is soft and golden. Cool garlic to room temperature.

Place garlic, lemon juice, and Worcestershire sauce in blender. Process until smooth. Add mayonnaise base, parsley, basil, and salt and pepper to taste to mixture. Process mixture until smooth.

TENDER BAR + KITCHEN

4300 BUTLER STREET
PITTSBURGH, PA 15201
(412) 402-9522
TENDERPGH.COM
OWNERS: JEFF AND ERIN CATALINA
CHEF: NEAL HEIDEKAT

Repurposing goods is a recent trend sweeping the nation. Barn wood is becoming tables. Coke bottles are becoming art pieces. And banks are becoming restaurants. Located in the Arsenal Bank Building, Tender Bar + Kitchen, named for the legal tender that once changed hands at the bank, is the second Pittsburgh restaurant from Jeff and Erin Catalina.

From 1884 to 1943, the beautiful red-brick building on the corner of Butler and 43rd Streets was home to Arsenal Bank. Now the building serves as a Prohibition-era cocktail lounge and restaurant. Playing off the building's character and history, much of the original interior charm was left intact or repurposed to help create the ambience. Marble from the wall was turned into the bar counter, checks were used as wallpaper, and six working safes all add to the authenticity of the concept.

With direction from Chef Neal Heidekat, Tender aims to celebrate America's unique regional quirks on the forever rotating small plates menu. Beef on weck from Buffalo, New York; shrimp and grits from Charleston, South Carolina; *poke* from Honolulu, Hawaii; and city chicken from Pittsburgh all make appearances. "It's all about education," says Neal. "It's one of the major missions here at Tender—to educate people not only about the food we do but also the history of American food."

Chef Neal is also devoted to being a scratch kitchen, making everything he possibly can in-house. Take the Fluffernutter from Massachusetts for example. Neal and his team make the brioche, peanut butter, marshmallow

(which is vegetarian!), and banana jam all in-house. The result is a savory sandwich that might evoke memories of your elementary lunchroom.

And let's not forget about the cocktails. Choose from Tender-created cocktails that are Bulls and Bears (stiff and straightforward), Luxuries (on the sweeter side), or Recovery Measures (refreshing and light). And gaze as the tenders of the bar carefully craft your cocktail choice. Thirty classic cocktails from the Banker's List such as the brandy milk punch and Death in the Afternoon, wines, draft beers and ciders, and phosphate sodas are also available to wet your whistle.

CITY CHICKEN

SERVES 8

For the brine (see note on page 184):

1 cup kosher salt
½ cup light brown sugar
1 large bay leaf
1 tablespoon whole black peppercorns
1 tablespoon dry rubbed sage
1 quart water

For the city chicken:

3 pounds pork tenderloin, cleaned and
    cut into 1-inch cubes

For the sauce:

5 pounds pork leg bones
2 pounds Spanish onions
1 pound carrots
1 pound celery
5 sprigs fresh thyme or 3 tablespoons dried thyme
5 sprigs flat-leaf parsley
2 tablespoons whole black peppercorns
3 large bay leaves
1 quart apple cider, simmered and reduced to 1 cup

For the breading:

2 cups flour
2 tablespoons kosher salt

1 tablespoon freshly ground black pepper
3 eggs
2 cups panko bread crumbs
¼ cup dry rubbed sage

Special equipment:

Thermometer
8 (8-inch) bamboo skewers, soaked in water
    for at least an hour

To prepare the brine: Combine all of the ingredients for the brine in a saucepan over medium heat. Bring the brine up to a simmer, stirring occasionally to dissolve the salt and sugar. After it simmers, remove from the heat and cool the brine to about 40°F; pour over cubed pork. Allow the pork to brine for at least 1 hour, but not more than 2 hours. After the pork is done brining, gently rinse the cubes under cold water and pat dry. (After you remove it from the brine, the pork can refrigerate overnight, if necessary, in a tightly sealed container; skewer and bread it the next day.)

To prepare the sauce: Preheat oven to 400°F. Place pork leg bones in a sturdy roasting pan and roast until nicely caramelized, starting your timer at 15 minutes and then checking every 2 to 3 minutes. After the bones are roasted, allow them

to cool. Place the bones in a large stockpot and fill it with water. The pot should be large enough to eventually accommodate all of the ingredients for the sauce (except the apple cider) plus 2 inches of water. Place the pot over medium heat and bring to just under a simmer. Continue to cook the contents at this temperature for 5 hours. Monitor the heat and skim the fat, purging it intermittently from the bones. After 5 hours,

add the onions, carrots, celery, thyme, parsley, peppercorns, and bay leaves. Cook for 1 more hour. Strain the stock and discard everything but the liquid. Clean the pot and put the strained stock back in. Return to medium heat and reduce to a simmer, still skimming any impurities, until the sauce is thick enough to coat the back of a metal spoon. This process may take a couple of hours. Add reduced apple cider to taste.

To prepare the breading: Set up four bowls or trays side by side. Make sure that the vessels of choice are large enough to accommodate the skewers and that you have plenty of room to work. In the first, combine the flour with the salt and pepper. In the second, beat the eggs thoroughly. In the third, combine the bread crumbs and sage. The fourth is to be used as a receptacle for the breaded skewers.

To prepare the city chicken: Preheat oven to 350°F. Skewer the pork, six cubes of pork to each 8-inch skewer. Lightly dredge the skewered pork in the seasoned flour, thoroughly coating the meat. Gently shake off any excess flour, then coat it in the beaten egg. Allow any excess egg to drip off, then transfer to the bread crumbs and bread thoroughly on all sides. Place the breaded pork on a rack that will allow air to flow around it in the oven. Bake pork for 20 minutes or until it reaches your desired level of doneness.

To serve: Tender recommends placing city chicken on a bed of mushroom mashed potatoes and drizzle sauce on chicken and around the plate.

Note from the chef: Chef Neal recommends making the brine and stock and reducing the cider the night before.

THE VAN BUREN
MAKES 1 COCKTAIL

1½ ounces gin (Wigle Genever preferred)
½ ounce green Chartreuse
½ ounce Bénédictine
½ ounce dry vermouth
Dash of rhubarb bitters (optional)
Ice
Rose water (optional)

Pour the gin, Chartreuse, Bénédictine, vermouth, and bitters into a cocktail shaker. Stir with ice. Strain into a rocks glass over large ice cubes or "rocks." Mist with rose water, if desired.

WHAT'S THE PASSWORD?

Alcohol is legal, but cocktail joints are turning the clocks back to Prohibition. The latest trend in craft cocktails: old-timey mixology. Bars around the 'Burgh are serving up classic drinks with flare (think jaunty caps, suspenders, handlebar mustaches) and attention paid to every ingredient. Bitters made in-house. Absinthe spritzed on glass rims. Basil hand crushed. No detail is left unexplored. These carefully crafted bevs take time to create, but the payoff sure is the bee's knees. Get a fancy drink at one of these spots, no password needed: Acacia, acaciacocktails.com; Bar Marco, barmarco.squarespace.com (page 14); Tender Bar + Kitchen, tenderpgh.com (page 181); Harvard & Highland, unionpgh.com; and Butterjoint, thebutterjoint.com (page 113).

TEPPANYAKI KYOTO

5808 BRYANT STREET
PITTSBURGH, PA 15206
(412) 441-1610
OWNER/CHEF: KEVIN CHEN
OWNER: SHIHO JINO

"It just is my happy," says Teppanyaki Kyoto's owner and chef, Kevin Chen. This source of happiness? Food of course. Inside his tranquil restaurant space along Bryant Street, Kevin provides diners a taste of bliss by way of traditional, Japanese comfort food.

"Most people think that Japanese cuisine is just fish or sushi," says Kevin. "I wanted to bring something different to Pittsburgh."

Kevin hails from Taiwan but has called Pittsburgh home for about a dozen years. During that time, he traveled to Kyoto, Japan, the restaurant's namesake and his wife and co-owner Shiho's hometown, to learn to cook. He brought a style of cooking back to the 'Burgh that is seen all over Kyoto—from street vendors to upscale restaurants.

Teppanyaki Kyoto is certainly unique in Pittsburgh's food landscape. The highlight of the sushi-free Japanese menu are the "pancakes": the Okonomiyaki and the Hiroshimayaki. These savory dishes have bases of cabbage batter and can contain a variety of options like shrimp, rice cakes,

and tofu. The names denote the style of preparation and regional origin: The Okonomiyaki (Osaka, Japan), ingredients are mixed together; the Hiroshimayaki (Hiroshima) is layered. Both are expertly crafted in the open kitchen complete with flat-top grill. Striving for authenticity, it helps that Kevin's wife is familiar with the cuisine: "She can tell me if I have to do something differently."

Kevin, who was once a computer engineer, didn't always dream of being a restaurateur. In fact, as a child, he longed to be a pilot. "But I couldn't fly because of my glasses," he laughs. Sure, he may not be steering an aircraft, but he flies diners' taste buds to Kyoto and back every night with the help of his culinary creations. Talk about a happy journey.

DASHI MAKI
SERVES 1

2 eggs
1 green onion, chopped
3 tablespoons plus 1 teaspoon dashi soup
   (1 teaspoon dashi powder mixed with
   6 tablespoons plus 2 teaspoons water)
5 teaspoons soy sauce
5 teaspoons Japanese mirin (sweet cooking wine)
2 tablespoons sesame oil

1 white radish, grated
Japanese sansho powder

Crack eggs in a bowl. Add green onion and mix.
Add cold dashi soup, soy sauce, and Japanese
mirin to eggs and mix.

Heat a frying pan. Spread a bit of oil in the frying
pan.

Pour the egg mixture into the frying pan. When
the mixture toughens, fold it over four times,
like an omelette. The egg mixture will be about
1½ x 3 inches in size.

To serve: Place the Dashi Maki on a plate.
Sprinkle with grated white radish and Japanese
sansho powder.

TSUKUNE

CHICKEN MEATBALLS

MAKES 20 MEATBALLS

For the sauce:

3 tablespoons Japanese mirin (sweet cooking wine)

3 tablespoons soy sauce

1 tablespoon granulated sugar

1½ tablespoons Japanese cooking sake

For the tsukune:

1 pound chicken thighs, ground

1 green onion, white part only, chopped

1 teaspoon grated ginger

3 teaspoons Japanese cooking sake

3 teaspoons potato starch

2 teaspoons soy sauce

3 teaspoons soy oil

Oil for cooking

To prepare the sauce: Mix mirin, soy sauce, sugar, and Japanese cooking sake together.

To prepare the tsukune: Combine ground chicken, green onion, grated ginger, Japanese cooking sake, potato starch, soy sauce, and soy oil together. Use your hands to mix the ingredients until they stick together and are thoroughly incorporated. Form into 1-inch balls.

Place tsukune in frying pan, pour oil on the top of meatballs, and cover. Using medium heat, cook for 3 minutes then flip meatballs and cook for another 3 minutes. Pour prepared sauce onto meatballs and continue cooking until well coated.

Thin Man Sandwich Shop

50 21st Street
Pittsburgh, PA 15222
(412) 586-7370
thinmansandwichshop.com
Chef/Owner: Dan and Sherri Leiphart

To some, sandwiches are the perfect canvas. Whether they're dressed up or dressed down, the result is usually the same: delicious. That blank canvas and general nature of the casually cool fare inspired husband-and-wife team Dan and Sherri Leiphart to open Thin Man Sandwich Shop.

Dan and Sherri met in culinary school and worked on and off at restaurants around the city, most recently sharing the title of co-executive chef at Isabela on Grandview. They decided to leave the fine dining world for a more casual and approachable atmosphere reflective of their personalities. Appreciative of the grandiose nature of upscale menus, Dan and Sherri wanted to provide the same quality at a much lower price point.

They opened the Thin Man Sandwich Shop in the epicenter of Pittsburgh food, the Strip District. The name isn't a reference to sandwich size but to the 1930s movie series *The Thin Man* about a husband-and-wife detective duo.

The menu at Thin Man is ingredient driven and actively supports the Pittsburgh community. Sometimes items will be available for a few months or only a few weeks, which means you'll have to make regular trips to ensure you get your favorites. Dan and Sherri also try to offer a balanced menu to appeal to all palates. You'll usually find vegetarian, fish, poultry, and beef options.

The best-selling sandwich is its namesake, The Thin Man. Chicken liver mousse, local bacon, frisée, and red wine vinaigrette on a baguette perfectly sums up what the two are trying to achieve with their first venture—high-end technique with flavors to introduce people to new tastes on the best canvas out there.

Braised Beef Shanks with Horseradish Mayonnaise, Whole Grain Mustard & Shaved Celery & Fennel

SERVES 4–6

For the horseradish mayonnaise:

2 egg yolks

1 teaspoon Dijon mustard

1 cup prepared horseradish, strained

2 teaspoons lemon juice

1 cup vegetable oil

Salt to taste

For the beef shanks:

2 pounds beef shank steaks

Salt and black pepper to taste

Canola oil for sautéing

1 large Spanish onion, cut into large dice

4 ounces carrots, cut into large dice

2 ribs celery, cut into large dice

1 tablespoon whole fennel seeds

1 thyme sprig

1 bay leaf

2 garlic cloves, smashed

4 whole black peppercorns

4 ounces Cabernet Sauvignon

4–6 cups water

4–6 (6-inch) baguettes

Whole grain mustard

Shaved celery

Shaved fennel

Special equipment:

Food processor

To prepare the horseradish mayonnaise: Put the egg yolks, mustard, and horseradish into a food processor and process for approximately 10 seconds. While processor is running, slowly stream in the lemon juice and oil to form an emulsion. Add salt and adjust to taste.

To prepare the beef shanks: Preheat the oven to 325°F.

Season the shanks aggressively with salt and black pepper. Heat a roasting pan over medium-high heat until very hot. Add canola oil and sear shanks on all sides until a crust forms (about 4 minutes per side).

Add the vegetables, herbs, and spices and sauté for another 2 to 3 minutes. Add the wine and just enough water to barely cover the shanks. Season the liquid with salt to taste. Cover the pan with foil and bring up to a boil.

Put the roasting pan into the preheated oven and braise for approximately 4½ hours. Check the pan every hour or so to make sure the liquid has not all evaporated and add more water if necessary. The beef is done when it falls away from the bone with little or no resistance. When the beef is cool enough to handle, gently separate the meat from the fat. Discard the fat.

Strain and reserve the braising liquid.

To assemble the sandwiches: Reheat the beef shank in the reserved braising liquid, allowing the liquid to reduce slightly. At the same time, cut the baguettes lengthwise and toast until just slightly crispy. Spread each baguette with 2 tablespoons of horseradish mayonnaise on the bottom and 1 tablespoon of whole grain mustard on the top. Place approximately 4 to 5 ounces of beef shank and about 1 tablespoon of braising liquid on the bottom half of each baguette.

Garnish with shaved celery and fennel.

PUMPKIN SOUP WITH WIGLE RYE WHISKEY, CRÈME FRAÎCHE & WHOLE GRAIN CROUTONS

SERVES 8–10

For the sachet:

4 black peppercorns, whole
¼ teaspoon crushed red pepper flakes
2 bay leaves
1 fresh thyme sprig

For the soup:

3 ounces carrots, peeled and cut into large dice
2 ribs celery, cut into large dice
1 small Spanish onion, cut into large dice
3 ounces shallots, peeled and sliced
2 garlic cloves, peeled and smashed
Canola oil for sautéing
2 pounds pumpkin, peeled and cut into large dice
    (small pie pumpkins)

2 quarts water
½ cup heavy cream
¼ cup honey
6 ounces Wigle Rye Whiskey
Salt and white pepper to taste

Crème fraîche for garnish
Whole grain croutons for garnish
Fresh chives for garnish

Special equipment:

Cheesecloth
Butcher's twine
Blender

To prepare the sachet: Wrap the peppercorns, red pepper flakes, bay leaves, and thyme in a piece of cheesecloth and tie tightly with butcher's twine.

To prepare the soup: In a large pot over medium-high heat, sauté the carrots, celery, onions, shallots, and garlic in a small amount of canola oil for approximately 2 to 3 minutes. Add the sachet and continue to sauté for another 2 to 3 minutes, or until the onions are translucent. Add the pumpkin and water and bring up to a boil. Turn the heat to simmer and cook until the pumpkin is soft, approximately 20 minutes. Remove the sachet.

Working in batches, puree the soup in a blender. Return the soup to the pot and stir in the heavy cream, honey, and whiskey. Adjust seasoning to taste.

To serve: Garnish with crème fraîche, whole grain croutons, and fresh chives.

Note from the chef: Be careful not to overfill the blender while working as the mixture is very hot and will produce steam inside the vessel. In place of blender, you may use an immersion blender directly in the pot.

Verde Mexican Kitchen & Cantina

5491 Penn Avenue
Pittsburgh, PA 15206
(412) 404-8487
verdepgh.com
Owners: Jeff and Erin Catalina
Chef: Lynette "LBEE" Bushey

Sometimes dreams do come true. And for Jeff and Erin Catalina, their dream came in the form of an upscale Mexican restaurant.

Originally from San Antonio, Texas, Jeff grew up indulging in a wide variety of Mexican cuisine. So when he and his wife moved to Pittsburgh, they sought out the same variety. When nothing fit the bill, they took matters into their own hands and opened Verde Mexican Kitchen & Cantina in Garfield.

The menu is made up of the traditional ingredients and flavors of Mexico but with a modern Verde twist. Before leading the kitchen at Verde, Chef Lynette "LBEE" Bushey spent seven years in Nicaragua at the Pelican Eyes Resort. And that knowledge and know-how is reflected in the menu.

Classic chili rellenos are reworked and include mushrooms, wild rice, Mexican cheeses, chipotle asado, and *samfaina*. Tacos are filled with ancho roasted Yukon Gold potatoes, roasted poblano chile strips, red cabbage, *queso fresco,* and *huitlacoche*

crema, or pan-seared chile-marinated mahimahi, poblano napa slaw, and chipotle aioli, among others.

Jeff is also passionate about craft cocktails, which isn't hard to see once you look at the drink menu. Verde has over two hundred varieties of tequila available to sample. Don't think quality is overlooked because of quantity. Fresh limes are squeezed continuously, syrups and infusions are made in-house, and drinks are featured seasonally.

The entire staff is extensively trained to help educate those indulging in Verde's spirit of choice whether you enjoy it straight up, in a craft cocktail, or in a tasting flight. Either ask the bartender or use the world's first tequila menu app to help narrow down your choices. Jeff's so enthralled by the spirit that he works with importers and sales representatives to introduce varieties not yet available in Pittsburgh to tequila enthusiasts.

MARIPOSA MARGARITA
MAKES 1 COCKTAIL

For the honey-orange-lavender syrup
  (makes about 3 cups of syrup):

1½ cups honey
1 cup water
½ cup sugar
1 ounce dried lavender flowers
1 full orange peel

For the margarita:

2 ounces tequila (Antiguo Reposado preferred)
1 ounce honey-orange-lavender syrup (see above)
½ ounce fresh-squeezed lime juice
Ice
Wide orange peel for garnish

To prepare the honey-orange-lavender syrup:
Combine the honey, water, sugar, dried lavender
flowers, and orange peel In saucepan and simmer
for 3 to 4 minutes. Remove from heat, cover with
lid, and steep for 15 minutes.

Pour liquid through wire-mesh strainer into a
container. Serve or store in an airtight container
in the refrigerator. The syrup can keep for up to a
month.

To prepare the margarita: Combine the tequila, the
honey-orange-lavender syrup, and lime juice in a
cocktail shaker with ice. Shake vigorously. Strain
and serve over ice in a rocks glass. Garnish with a
wide orange peel.

TOMATILLO SALSA
MAKES 2 QUARTS

2 pounds fresh tomatillos, husked and washed
1 small white onion
1 poblano pepper, with seeds
2 jalapeños, with seeds
1 green pepper, without seeds
4 garlic cloves
1 bunch fresh cilantro leaves
Juice of 1 lime
2 tablespoons Frank's Red Hot
2 teaspoons cayenne pepper
½ tablespoon ground black pepper
1 tablespoon salt
3 tablespoons granulated sugar

Special equipment:

Blender

Preheat oven to 450°F.

Roast tomatillos for 20 to 30 minutes or until
tomatillos are slightly charred. While tomatillos are
roasting, clean and roughly chop the white onion,
poblano pepper, jalapeños, green pepper, garlic,
and cilantro. Put the roughly chopped ingredients
into blender. Puree until smooth. Once smooth,
add roasted tomatillos to blender. Puree to desired
consistency. Remove from blender and mix in lime
juice, hot sauce, cayenne pepper, black pepper,
salt, and sugar. Mix until completely Incorporated.

Once combined, refrigerate in a sealed container
for a few hours to allow all the flavors to blend.

Note from the chef: Refrigerate any leftovers and
use within 7 days.

Waffles INCaffeinated

2517 East Carson Street
Pittsburgh, PA 15203
(412) 301-1763
facebook.com/WafflesINCaffeinated
Chef/Owner: Tahj Merriman
Owners: Cassandra and Josh Cuddy, Gordon Sheffer

"I owe most of my career to cinnamon toast," jokes Tahj Merriman, chef and co-owner of the South Side's Waffle INCaffeinated. He began making cinnamon toast in his kitchen at the age of six. Young Tahj dabbled in other combinations of food like tuna and soda pop. "Take it from me, that is not a good choice."

Tahj started his true culinary career apprenticing at the historic Greenbrier resort in West Virginia and then making sushi in Japan. After a couple other stints across the country, he decided to move back home to start his own business in Beaver County, Pennsylvania.

So what to make? Not cinnamon toast, but Tahj did stick with classic breakfast fare: waffles. "Growing up, we used to eat waffles every weekend," says Tahj. "Waffles are a comfort food. I felt like I could put my own spin on it, without alienating anyone."

With a lease agreement dictating that the waffle restaurant had to make thirty-six dozen doughnuts per day and some tough business sledding, the first iteration of Waffles INCaffeinated was short lived. Tahj enlisted and completed basic training before giving the restaurant another go.

"I joined the army to take a break," laughs Tahj. "Restaurants are definitely more stressful."

Currently on active duty, Tahj was able to resurrect Waffles INCaffeinated in New Brighton, Pennsylvania, and on Pittsburgh's South Side by partnering with his cousin Cassandra Cuddy, her husband and Tahj's army mate Josh, and Gordon Sheffer.

The waffles, infused with Tahj's creativity and a hint of grandma's secret recipe and sourdough, are topped or mixed with berries, ham, walnuts . . . and the list goes on and on. Other breakfast options, like omelettes and pancakes, are available, as well as lunch plates. It is a good place to take a break and enjoy a full service, freshly prepared breakfast.

THE BENNY

WAFFLES BENEDICT

SERVES 8

For the hollandaise:

1 pound (4 sticks) unsalted sweet cream butter

1 teaspoon kosher salt

4 eggs

2 tablespoons lemon juice

½ teaspoon Tabasco or hot sauce

1 teaspoon Worcestershire sauce

½ teaspoon salt

½ teaspoon ground white pepper

For the poached eggs:

2 cups cider vinegar per gallon of water

8 eggs

8 slices ham or Canadian bacon

2 cooked waffles, quartered

8 ounces lump crabmeat

¼ cup chopped green onion

Special equipment

Thermometer

Kitchen scale

To make the hollandaise sauce: Begin by clarifying the butter. To clarify, melt over medium heat and spoon away half of the milk fat. Leaving in half of the milk fat gives the hollandaise a fluffier consistency. Keep the temperature at 120°F to 140°F.

Bring salt and a pan of water to a boil. Separate 4 eggs, placing the yolks into a stainless steel bowl. Add lemon juice to the yolks and whisk until combined. Place the bowl over the simmering water, not letting the water touch the bowl. Whisk vigorously until soft peaks are formed. Make sure to not cook the eggs over 120°F.

Remove the bowl from heat and whisk in 2 tablespoons of clarified butter to start. Once the emulsion begins to hold together, add butter at a steadier pace. If the mixture appears greasy, stir until combined, while adding more butter. Add the Tabasco, Worcestershire sauce, and salt and pepper to taste.

To poach the eggs: Bring water to a boil and add vinegar. Drop eggs in, one at a time, by first cracking each egg separately into a small bowl before adding to water. Cook each egg for 3 minutes.

While the eggs are poaching, warm the ham in a pan and place on top of waffle quarter.

To serve: Place a poached egg on top of the ham and ladle on the hollandaise. Add 1 ounce crabmeat to each quarter and garnish with chopped green onion.

WINGHART'S BURGER & WHISKEY BAR

DOWNTOWN
5 MARKET SQUARE
PITTSBURGH, PA 15222
(412) 434-5600

SOUTH SIDE
1505 EAST CARSON STREET
PITTSBURGH, PA 15203
(412) 904-4620
WINGHARTBURGERS.COM
CHEF/OWNER: ZACHERY WINGHART

How do you make the perfect hamburger? Zachery Winghart, chef and owner of Winghart's Burger & Whiskey Bar, says it starts with the meat. "We only use one cut of meat. We don't do a blend. Chuck roll is literally the best cut of meat for making hamburgers because it still has that texture and springiness and density that you want in a hamburger." The quality and freshness is so important that the certified butcher freshly grinds his choice cut of meat each day at his South Side location.

Zachery started his culinary career in the world of fine dining, working and learning from master chefs up and down the East Coast. Once he was back in Pittsburgh, he took on an apprenticeship as a butcher, mastering how to break down whole cows. Then one night he had a dream, called his business partner at 2:30 a.m., and soon after opened the first Winghart's in Market Square.

The personality at Winghart's is completely different than Zachery's fine-dining background. You won't find white tablecloths, a monochromatic uniformed waitstaff, or a stiff buttoned-up ambience. You'll find the exact opposite: genuine and unique personalities serving the best possible meal they can regardless of who you are.

"Food can literally change someone's day. Winghart's is about the customer experience. It's a real restaurant with no glitz and glamour. It just is what it is," says Zachery.

The menu at Winghart's is another expression of personality. Over a few bottles of wine, Zachery and several friends developed the first menu. The featured burgers are inspired and named after people in Zachery's life. One that especially makes Zachery light up is Harper's Fairly Good Burger, named for his son. With Boursin cheese, pancetta, crispy shoestring onions, and bordelaise sauce, it's more than "fairly good." Another crowd favorite is the Shipwreck Burger, named for Zachery's close bud Shipwreck: Brie cheese, caramelized onions with bacon, arugula, and white truffle aioli ooze together on top of that freshly ground burger.

The perfect hamburger is different for everyone. It comes in all shapes and flavors. But one thing's for sure: If you're at Winghart's, the perfect hamburger starts with the meat.

SHIPWRECK BURGER

SERVES 4

For the burger:

2 pounds ground chuck (ask butcher to grind from the roast)
Salt and pepper to taste

For the white truffle aioli:

1 cup mayonnaise
2 tablespoons white truffle oil
2 cloves garlic, roasted and crushed

For the caramelized onions:

¼ pound (1 stick) unsalted butter
2 large white onions, peeled and julienned
Salt to taste

4 buns of your choice
4 ounces brie cheese, sliced
8 slices bacon, cooked
Handful of arugula

Special equipment:

Cast iron griddle (optional)

To prepare the burger: Form the ground chuck into ¼-pound patties. Season with salt and pepper to taste. Cook or grill patties to desired temperature. Use a cast iron griddle, if possible, to caramelize the protein.

To prepare the white truffle aioli: Combine mayonnaise, white truffle oil, and crushed garlic in a bowl and whisk together.

To prepare the caramelized onions: Combine butter, white onions, and salt in a saucepan over low heat. Cook until onions are dark brown.

To assemble the burger: Place the cooked burger patty on the bottom bun. Spread the aioli on the top half of each bun. Stack the ingredients in the following order: brie, caramelized onions, bacon, arugula. Roll up your sleeves and enjoy!

Index

About the Authors & Photographer

Authors pictured left to right: Laura Zorch, Sarah Sudar, Amanda McFadden, and Julia Gongaware

Laura Zorch once ate a pound of chocolate in fifteen minutes. She writes from her Pittsburgh home, where she also indulges in her favorite pastime of decorating cakes with hilarious phrasing. She has never met a shark, but it is on her life list, along with learning a new language, joining a band, and enjoying a steak dinner with a professional hockey player.

Sarah Sudar is a Pittsburgh-based writer who is obsessed with eating cupcakes and listening to hip-hop music, often at the same time. She holds a bachelor's degree in business administration from the University of Pittsburgh and a master's in journalism from Point Park University. When she's not organizing her life into spreadsheets, she can be found window-shopping for designer handbags and studying up on the etiquette rules of the early 1880s.

Amanda McFadden can survive on only ice cream for days. She calls Pittsburgh home but dreams of one day sailing 'round the world or ranching it up with a handsome cowboy. When she isn't writing, she's taking in a concert, a baseball game, or an entire pizza. Mandy loves drinking at brunch, reading halfway through Hemingway novels, and pretending she can play the guitar.

Julia Gongaware is a food writer from Pittsburgh who dances to Michael Jackson in front of her bedroom mirror when no one is looking. She hates grape-flavored candy but loves drawing pictures of strangers. Right now she's probably listening to Justin Timberlake while scouring Pinterest for DIY projects she'll never actually do.

Cayla Zahoran is a Pittsburgh-based photographer who specializes in not only photographing food but eating it, too. She graduated from the Art Institute of Pittsburgh with an associate's degree in photography. In her spare time, you can find her browsing antique malls and thrift stores, buying things no one else wants.